60th Annual Meeting of the Association for Computational Linguistics (ACL 2022)

Tutorial Abstracts

Dublin, Ireland
22-27 May 2022

ISBN: 978-1-7138-6725-8

Printed from e-media with permission by:

Curran Associates, Inc.
57 Morehouse Lane
Red Hook, NY 12571

proceedings.com

Some format issues inherent in the e-media version may also appear in this print version.

Printed with permission by Curran Associates, Inc. (2023)

For permission requests, please contact the Association for Computational Linguistics
at the address below.

Association for Computational Linguistics
209 N. Eighth Street
Stroudsburg, Pennsylvania 18360

Phone: 1-570-476-8006
Fax: 1-570-476-0860

acl@aclweb.org

Additional copies of this publication are available from:

Curran Associates, Inc.
57 Morehouse Lane
Red Hook, NY 12571 USA
Phone: 845-758-0400
Fax: 845-758-2633
Email: curran@proceedings.com
Web: www.proceedings.com

ACL 2022

The 60th Annual Meeting of the Association for Computational Linguistics

Tutorial Abstracts

May 22-27, 2022

Introduction

Welcome to the Tutorials Session of ACL 2022.

The ACL tutorials session is organized to give conference attendees a comprehensive introduction by expert researchers to some topics of importance drawn from our rapidly growing and changing research field.

This year, as has been the tradition over the past few years, the call, submission, reviewing and selection of tutorials were coordinated jointly for multiple conferences: ACL, NAACL, COLING and EMNLP. We formed a review committee of 34 members, including the ACL tutorial chairs (Luciana Benotti (then), Naoaki Okazaki, and Marcos Zampieri), the NAACL tutorial chairs (Cecilia O. Alm, Yulia Tsetkov, and Miguel Ballesteros), the COLING tutorial chairs (Heng Ji, Hsin-Hsi Chen, and Lucia Donatelli), the EMNLP tutorial chairs (Samhaa R. El-Beltagy and Xipeng Qiu), and 23 external reviewers (see Program Committee for the full list). A reviewing process was organised so that each proposal received 3 reviews. The selection criteria included clarity and preparedness, novelty or timely character of the topic, instructors' experience, likely audience interest, open access of the tutorial instructional material, and diversity and inclusion. A total of 47 tutorial submissions were received, of which 8 were selected for presentation at ACL.

We solicited two types of tutorials, namely cutting-edge themes and introductory themes. The 8 tutorials for ACL include 2 introductory tutorials and 6 cutting-edge tutorials. The introductory tutorials are dedicated to deep neural networks and reproducibility in NLP. The cutting-edge discussions address knowledge-augmented methods, non-autoregressive sequence generation, learning with limited data, zero- and few-shot learning with pretrained language models, vision-language pretraining, and multilingual task-oriented dialogue.

We would like to thank the tutorial authors for their contributions and flexibility while organising the conference in the hybrid mode. We are also grateful to the 23 external reviewers for their generous help in the decision process. Our thanks go to the conference organizers for effective collaboration, and in particular to the general chair Bernardo Magnini, the publication chair Danilo Croce, the handbook chair Marco Polignano, and the authors of `aclpub2`. Finally, special thanks go to Luciana Benotti, who worked hard as a tutorial chair of ACL especially maintaining the reviewing process (including the administrative work with OpenReview) but later resigned from this position when she was elected to the NAACL executive board as the NAACL chair for 2022.

We hope you enjoy the tutorials.

ACL 2022 Tutorial Co-chairs
Luciana Benotti (until Jan 2022)
Naoaki Okazaki
Yves Scherrer
Marcos Zampieri

Organizing Committee

General Chair

Bernardo Magnini, FBK, Italy

Program Chairs

Smaranda Muresan, Columbia University, USA
Preslav Nakov, Qatar Computing Research Institute, HBKU, Qatar
Aline Villavicencio, University of Sheffield, UK

Tutorial Chairs

Luciana Benotti (until Jan 2022), National University of Córdoba, Argentina
Naoaki Okazaki, Tokyo Institute of Technology, Japan
Yves Scherrer, University of Helsinki, Finland
Marcos Zampieri, Rochester Institute of Technology, USA

Program Committee

Program Committee

Cecilia Alm, Rochester Institute of Technology, USA
Antonios Anastasopoulos, George Mason University, USA
Miguel Ballesteros, Amazon, USA
Daniel Beck, University of Melbourne, Australia
Luciana Benotti, National University of Córdoba, Argentina
Yevgeni Berzak, Technion, Israel Institute of Technology, Israel
Erik Cambria, Nanyang Technological University, Singapore
Hsin-Hsi Chen, National Taiwan University, Taiwan
Gaël Dias, University of Caen Normandy, France
Lucia Donatelli, Saarland University, Germany
Samhaa R. El-Beltagy, Newgiza University, Egypt
Karën Fort, Sorbonne Université / LORIA, France
Heng Ji, University of Illinois, Urbana-Champaign, USA
David Jurgens, University of Michigan, USA
Naoaki Okazaki, Tokyo Institute of Technology, Japan
Alexis Palmer, University of Colorado, Boulder, USA
Mohammad Taher Pilehvar, Tehran Institute for Advanced Studies, Iran
Barbara Plank, LMU Munich, Germany and IT University of Copenhagen, Denmark
Emily Prud'hommeaux, Boston College, USA
Xipeng Qiu, Fudan University, China
Agata Savary, Université Paris-Saclay, France
João Sedoc, New York University, USA
Yulia Tsvetkov, University of Washington, USA
Aline Villavicencio, University of Sheffield, UK
Ivan Vulić, University of Cambridge, UK
Yogarshi Vyas, Amazon, USA
Joachim Wagner, Dublin City University, Ireland
Taro Watanabe, Nara Institute of Science and Technology, Japan
Aaron Steven White, University of Rochester, USA
Diyi Yang, Georgia Institute of Technology, USA
Marcos Zampieri, Rochester Institute of Technology, USA
Meishan Zhang, Harbin Institute of Technology (Shenzhen), China
Yue Zhang, Westlake University, China
Arkaitz Zubiaga, Queen Mary University London, UK

Table of Contents

A Gentle Introduction to Deep Nets and Opportunities for the Future
Kenneth Church, Valia Kordoni, Gary Marcus, Ernest Davis, Yanjun Ma and Zeyu Chen 1

Towards Reproducible Machine Learning Research in Natural Language Processing
Ana Lucic, Maurits Bleeker, Samarth Bhargav, Jessica Zosa Forde, Koustuv Sinha, Jesse Dodge, Sasha Luccioni and Robert Stojnic 7

Knowledge-Augmented Methods for Natural Language Processing
Chenguang Zhu, Yichong Xu, Xiang Ren, Bill Yuchen Lin, Meng Jiang and Wenhao Yu 12

Non-Autoregressive Sequence Generation
Jiatao Gu and Xu Tan 21

Learning with Limited Text Data
Diyi Yang, Ankur P Parikh and Colin Raffel 28

Zero- and Few-Shot NLP with Pretrained Language Models
Iz Beltagy, Arman Cohan, Robert L. Logan IV, Sewon Min and Sameer Singh 32

Vision-Language Pretraining: Current Trends and the Future
Aishwarya Agrawal, Damien Teney and Aida Nematzadeh 38

Natural Language Processing for Multilingual Task-Oriented Dialogue
Evgeniia Razumovskaia, Goran Glavaš, Olga Majewska, Edoardo Ponti and Ivan Vulić 44

A Gentle Introduction to Deep Nets and Opportunities for the Future

Kenneth Church
Baidu, Sunnyvale, USA
Kenneth.Ward.Church@gmail.com

Valia Kordoni
Humboldt-Universitaet zu Berlin, Germany
evangelia.kordoni@anglistik.hu-berlin.de

Gary Marcus
NYU & Robust.AI
gary.marcus@icloud.com

Ernest Davis
New York University
davise@cims.nyu.edu

Yanjun Ma & Zeyu Chen
Baidu, Beijing, China
mayanjun02@baidu.com

Abstract

The first half of this tutorial will make deep nets more accessible to a broader audience, following "Deep Nets for Poets" and "A Gentle Introduction to Fine-Tuning." We will also introduce, *gft* (general fine tuning), a little language for fine tuning deep nets with short (one line) programs that are as easy to code as regression in statistics packages such as R using glm (general linear models). Based on the success of these methods on a number of benchmarks, one might come away with the impression that deep nets are all we need. However, we believe the glass is half-full: while there is much that can be done with deep nets, there is always more to do. The second half of this tutorial will discuss some of these opportunities.

1 Introduction

This tutorial is split into two parts:

A Glass is half-full: deep nets can do much
B Glass is half-empty: there is always more to do

Part A will make deep nets more accessible to a broader audience (Church et al., 2021b,a) by introducing *gft* (General Fine-Tuning), a new "little language"[1] for deep nets that is similar to *glm* (general linear models) in the statistics package R.[2] *gft* code will be posted on the tutorial website.[3]

2 Part A: Glass is Half-Full

2.1 The Standard Recipe

Following (Devlin et al., 2019; Howard and Ruder, 2018), it has become standard practice to use the 3-step recipe in Table 1, with an emphasis on pre-trained (foundation/base) models (Bommasani et al., 2021). *gft* prefers the terms, *fit* and *predict*, which have a long tradition in statistics, and predate relatively recent work on deep nets.

Step	*gft*	Standard Terminology
1		Pre-Training
2	fit	Fine-Tuning
3	predict	Inference

Table 1: 3-Step recipe has become standard practice

gft makes it easy to use models and datasets on hubs: HuggingFace[4] and PaddleHub/PaddleNLP.[5] The hubs are large (30k models and 3k datasets), and growing quickly (3x/year). The challenge is to make these amazing resources more accessible to a diverse user-base. One does not need to know python and machine learning to use an off-the-shelf regression package. So too, deep nets should not require much (if any) programming skills.

2.2 Examples of Fit (aka Fine-Tuning)

Fit takes a pre-trained model, f_{pre} (BERT), and uses a dataset (emotion) to output a post-trained model, f_{post} (to $outdir):

```
gft_fit --data "H:emotion" \
    --model "H:bert-base-cased" \
    --eqn "classify:label~text" \
    --output_dir "$outdir"
```

Listing 1: Example of *gft_fit*

The next example is similar but uses a model and a dataset from PaddleNLP. *gft* supports mixing and matching models and datasets from different hubs.

```
gft_fit --data "P:chnsenticorp" \
    --model "P:ernie-tiny" \
    --eqn "classify:label~text" \
    --output_dir "$outdir"
```

Listing 2: H and P refer to HuggingFace and PaddleNLP

[1] Little languages were advocated by Bentley (1986) and the Unix group. Little languages such as AWK (Aho et al., 1987) make it easy to solve remarkably powerful tasks with short (often one-line) programs.

[2] https://www.r-project.org/

[3] https://github.com/kwchurch/ACL2022_deepnets_tutorial

[4] https://huggingface.co/

[5] https://github.com/PaddlePaddle

Proceedings of the 60th Annual Meeting of the Association for Computational Linguistics: Tutorial Abstracts, pages 1 - 6
May 22-27, 2022 ©2022 Association for Computational Linguistics

–data arg	–eqn arg
H:glue,cola	classify: label ~ sentence
H:glue,sst2	classify: label ~ sentence
H:glue,wnli	classify: label ~sentence
H:glue,mrpc	classify: label ~ sentence1 + sentence2
H:glue,rte	classify: label ~sentence1 + sentence2
H:glue,qnli	classify: label ~ question + sentence
H:glue,qqp	classify: label ~question1 + question2
H:glue,sstb	regress: label ~sentence1 + sentence2
H:glue,mnli	classify: label ~ premise + hypothesis

Table 2: *gft* solutions for GLUE (Wang et al., 2018)

–data arg	–eqn arg
squad	classify_spans: answers ~ question + context
tweet_eval,hate	classify: label ~ text
conll2003	classify_tokens: pos_tags ~ tokens
conll2003	classify_tokens: ner_tags ~ tokens
conll2003	classify_tokens: chunk_tags ~ tokens
timit_asr	ctc: text ~ audio

Table 3: *gft* solutions for more benchmarks

Short (1-line) gft programs can fit (fine-tune) many benchmarks, as illustrated in Tables 2-3.

2.3 gft Cheatsheet

gft supports the following functions:

1. *fit* (*aka* fine-tuning): $f_{pre} + data \rightarrow f_{post}$
2. *predict* (*aka* inference): $f(x) = \hat{y}$, where x is an input from a dataset or from *stdin*
3. *eval*: $f + data \rightarrow score$
4. *summary*: search hubs for popular datasets, models and tasks, and provide snippets.
5. *cat_data*: output dataset on *stdout*

There are four major arguments:

1. –data: a dataset on a hub, or a local file
2. –model: a model on a hub, or a local file
3. –task: e.g., classify, regress[6]
4. –eqn (e.g., classify:$y \sim x_1+x_2$), where a task appears before the colon, and variables refer to columns in the dataset.

The *gft* interpreter is based on examples from hubs.[7] [8] Hubs encourage users to modify 500+ lines of pytorch as necessary if they want to change models, datasets and/or tasks. *gft* generalizes the examples so users can do much of that in a single line of *gft* code (with comparable performance).[9]

2.4 Some Simple Examples

2.4.1 Search

As mentioned above, users are overwhelmed with an embarrassment of riches. How do we find the good stuff on the hubs? The following outputs snippets for datasets, models and tasks:

```
m=bhadresh-savani/roberta-base-emotion
gft_summary --data "H:emotion"
gft_summary --model "H:$m"
gft_summary --task "H:classify"
```

Listing 3: Models/datasets/tasks → snippets

Search for datasets and models that contain the substring: *emotion*, sorted by downloads:

```
query=H:__contains__emotion
gft_summary --data "$query" --topn 5
gft_summary --model "$query" --topn 5
```

Listing 4: Searching for best *emotion* models/datasets

To find the most downloaded datasets and models, set the query to the empty string:

```
query=H:__contains__
gft_summary --data "$query" --topn 5
gft_summary --model "$query" --topn 5
```

Listing 5: Searching for best of everything

2.4.2 Predict (*aka* Inference)

After having found the *good* stuff, how do we use it? *gft_predict* takes input, x, from stdin and outputs predictions, $\hat{y}$.

```
c=H:classify
tc=H:token-classification
# sentiment classification
echo "I love you"|gft_predict --task $c
# emotion classification
echo "I love you"|
  gft_predict --task $c --model $m
# NER (Named Entity Recognition)
echo "I love New York"|
  gft_predict --task $tc
```

[6] Currently supported tasks are: classify (*aka* text-classification), classify_tokens (*aka* token-classification), classify_spans (*aka* QA, question-answering), classify_images (*aka* image-classification), classify_audio (*aka* audio-classification), regress, text-generation, MT (*aka* translation), ASR (*aka* ctc, automatic-speech-recognition), fill-mask. Tasks in parentheses are aliases.

[7] https://github.com/huggingface/transformers/blob/master/examples/pytorch/

[8] https://github.com/PaddlePaddle/PaddleNLP/tree/develop/examples

[9] *gft* supports most of the arguments in the examples on the hubs, so it is possible to tune hyperparameters such as batch size, learning rate and stopping rules. Tuning is important for SOTA-chasing (Church and Kordoni, 2022), though default settings are recommended for most users who prefer results that are easy to replicate, and reasonably competitive.

```
# cloze task (fill in the <mask>)
echo "I <mask> you"|
  gft_predict --task H:fill-mask
```

Listing 6: Examples of *gft_predict*

gft_predict can also input from a dataset split, and outputs a prediction, $\hat{y}$, for each x in the split:

```
eqn="classify:label~text"
gft_predict --eqn "$eqn" --model $m \
   --data H:emotion --split test
```

Listing 7: Input from a dataset (instead of *stdin*)

2.4.3 Evaluation

If we replace *gft_predict* (above) with *gft_eval* (below), then we obtain a single score (instead of a $\hat{y}$ for each x):

```
gft_eval --eqn "$eqn" --model $m \
   --data H:emotion --split test
```

Listing 8: Evaluating a model on a dataset

2.4.4 Ease of Use, Popularity & SOTA

Given an embarrassment of riches, how do we choose the best model? The literature emphasizes SOTA (state-of-the-art), hubs reward downloads, and *gft* advocates ease-of-use.

Table 4 reports accuracy for a few models containing "MRPC,"[10] as well as two custom models. *gft* makes it easy to achieve competitive results, close to distilbert (compressed) models. One can outperform models on the hubs, by tuning hyperparameters as Yuchen Bian did. Tuning is possible in *gft* (but not recommended), as discussed in footnote 9. The validation accuracy in Table 4 are well below test accuracy in Table 5,[11] [12] suggesting that popular/easy-to-use/compressed models are well below SOTA (though we should not compare validation accuracy with test accuracy).

2.5 Conclusions to Part A

Higher level (little) languages like *gft* have many advantages over examples found on hubs: short (1-line) programs are easier to read and write, more transparent and more portable (across hubs). *gft* code and hundreds of examples can be found on the tutorial website (see footnote 3).

[10] We tested 22 models from HuggingFace and 135 models from Yuchen Bian (personal communication). To save space, results are reported for the best of Bian's models, the top 3 HuggingFace models, and models with 100+ downloads.

[11] https://paperswithcode.com/sota/semantic-textual-similarity-on-mrpc

[12] https://gluebenchmark.com/leaderboard

Model	VAcc	D
C:RoBERTa large, tuned by Yuchen Bian	0.924	
H:textattack/roberta-base-MRPC	0.912	1623
H:textattack/albert-base-v2-MRPC	0.897	175
H:mrm8488/deberta-v3-small-finetuned-mrpc	0.892	30
H:textattack/bert-base-uncased-MRPC	0.877	10,133
H:textattack/distilbert-base-uncased-MRPC	0.858	108
H:ajrae/bert-base-uncased-finetuned-mrpc	0.858	115
C:*gft_fit* example (BERT with no tuning)	0.853	
H:textattack/distilbert-base-cased-MRPC	0.784	122

Table 4: *gft* achieves VAcc (accuracy on validation split) close to distilbert (compressed) models. HuggingFace models were selected using *gft_summary* to find popular models by downloads (D).

Source	Test Accuracy
GLUE Leaderboard (L)	0.945
Papers with code (PWC)	0.937
Human Baseline (HB)	0.863

Table 5: SOTA (state-of-the-art) for MRPC (GLUE). See footnote 11 for PWC, and 12 for L & HB.

The point of Part A is to demystify deep nets. No one would suggest that regression-like methods are magical, or even artificially intelligent.

The point of Part B is to set appropriate expectations. There are many classic problems in knowledge representation, cognitive science and linguistics that go beyond regression-like methods discussed in Part A.

3 Part B: Opportunities for Improvement

Language models (LMs) are based on (Firth, 1957): "You shall know a word by the company it keeps" and Zellig Harris's (1954) "distributional hypothesis." By construction, this approach learns many aspects of language, some more desirable (fluency, collocations, word patterns) and some less desirable (*biases* (Bender et al., 2021)). However, there are many aspects that are not learned: *truth* (logical form, temporal/spatial logic and possible worlds), *meaning*, *purpose* (planning (Kautz et al., 1986; Litman and Allen, 1987), discourse structure) and *commonsense knowledge* (time and space). These topics have been studied for decades in AI and knowledge representation and for centuries in linguistics and philosophy.

3.1 Truth

> To the extent that a use case places importance on the truth of the outputs provided, it is not a good fit for GPT-3 (Dale, 2021)

LMs have a tendency to "hallucinate" when summarizing documents. The output sounds plausible, but may add embellishments to the input. More generally, LMs tend to make up "alternative facts" faster than they can be fact-checked. This may well be their most dangerous failing; people might believe some of these conspiracy theories.

3.2 Meaning

A vivid example of challenges with meaning is Ettinger's (2020) study of negation. If you ask BERT to fill in the blank in:

- A robin is a ____ .
- A robin is not a ____.

the top answer is: "bird," in both cases. There are few wrong answers in the second case, but "bird" is one of them.

3.3 Purpose, Planning & Document Structure

LMs generate text word-by-word without looking ahead and thinking about the larger picture. Short outputs are remarkably fluent, but longer outputs tend to meander aimlessly. Dialogue systems optimize for smoothness from the most recent turn. Such short-term thinking may not be helpful to the user (Grice, 1975). In one notorious case, a GPT-3 chatbot in the medical domain advised a patient to commit suicide (Rousseau and Baudelaire, 2020). More generally, LMs produce non-sequiturs, contradictions, tautologies, echolalia (Metz, 2020).

3.4 Commonsense knowledge

Commonsense knowledge is basic knowledge of how the world works (Davis and Marcus, 2015). We tested GPT-3's command of spatial and temporal knowledge with questions such as:

Time: Who came first, Thomas Jefferson or John F. Kennedy?

Space: Which is further from Liverpool, England: Brussels, Belgium or Portland, Oregon?

GPT-3 performed at chance on space, and only slightly better on time. LMs can output dates for historical figures and coordinates of cities, if asked directly, but LMs struggle to use this knowledge for questions such as the ones above.

The questions in our experiment involve particularly simple forms of temporal and spatial reasoning. Many texts make use of complex temporal relations such as possible worlds[13] and hypothetical events (such as planning, hoping, fearing, and preventing) (Gordon and Hobbs, 2017). Text often make use of complex features involving shapes and spatial relations (Davis, 2013).

Time[14] and space (Bloom, 1999) have been extensively studied in linguistics and philosophy. It is natural to model time based on tense. One approach,[15] starts with speech time, S, reference time, R, and event time, E.[16]

past perfect (*had slept*) $E < R < S$
simple past (*slept*) $E \approx R, E < S, R < S$

There are also natural connections between linguistic constructions such as subjunctive (*would, could, should*) and possible worlds. More generally, much of the work in linguistics assumes a rich set of connections between surface representations (syntax) and deeper structures (semantics/pragmatics).

4 Conclusions: Some Paths Forward

Some of these opportunities can be addressed by relatively easy patches to Firth-based methods. For example, biases can be mitigated in the short term by vetting the training corpus (Hovy and Prabhumoye, 2021). Similarly, penalty terms can be added to the objective function to discourage hallucinations (Durmus et al., 2020). Fine-tuning on a corpus of commonsense knowledge can help with violations of commonsense (Zhang et al., 2021).

In the long term, it may be helpful to consider more radical alternatives (Marcus and Davis, 2019). Part A described some recent advances that have been remarkably successful, though to make long term advances beyond that, it may be necessary to take advantage of more diverse interdisciplinary approaches that include Firth-based methods, as well as decades of work on Knowledge Representation in AI, and centuries of work in linguistics and philosophy.

[13] `https://plato.stanford.edu/entries/possible-worlds/`

[14] `https://plato.stanford.edu/entries/logic-temporal/`

[15] `https://plato.stanford.edu/entries/reichenbach/#AxiTheRel192`

[16] In the past perfect, event time precedes reference time, which precedes speech time. In contrast, in the simple past, event time coincides with reference time, while both precede speech time.

References

Alfred V Aho, Brian W Kernighan, and Peter J Weinberger. 1987. *The AWK programming language*. Addison-Wesley Longman Publishing Co., Inc.

Emily M Bender, Timnit Gebru, Angelina McMillan-Major, and Shmargaret Shmitchell. 2021. On the dangers of stochastic parrots: Can language models be too big? In *Proceedings of the 2021 ACM Conference on Fairness, Accountability, and Transparency*, pages 610–623.

Jon Louis Bentley. 1986. Little languages. *Commun. ACM*, 29(8):711–721.

Paul Bloom. 1999. *Language and space*. MIT press.

Rishi Bommasani, Drew A. Hudson, Ehsan Adeli, Russ Altman, Simran Arora, Sydney von Arx, Michael S. Bernstein, Jeannette Bohg, Antoine Bosselut, Emma Brunskill, Erik Brynjolfsson, Shyamal Buch, Dallas Card, Rodrigo Castellon, Niladri Chatterji, Annie Chen, Kathleen Creel, Jared Quincy Davis, Dora Demszky, Chris Donahue, Moussa Doumbouya, Esin Durmus, Stefano Ermon, John Etchemendy, Kawin Ethayarajh, Li Fei-Fei, Chelsea Finn, Trevor Gale, Lauren Gillespie, Karan Goel, Noah Goodman, Shelby Grossman, Neel Guha, Tatsunori Hashimoto, Peter Henderson, John Hewitt, Daniel E. Ho, Jenny Hong, Kyle Hsu, Jing Huang, Thomas Icard, Saahil Jain, Dan Jurafsky, Pratyusha Kalluri, Siddharth Karamcheti, Geoff Keeling, Fereshte Khani, Omar Khattab, Pang Wei Kohd, Mark Krass, Ranjay Krishna, Rohith Kuditipudi, Ananya Kumar, Faisal Ladhak, Mina Lee, Tony Lee, Jure Leskovec, Isabelle Levent, Xiang Lisa Li, Xuechen Li, Tengyu Ma, Ali Malik, Christopher D. Manning, Suvir Mirchandani, Eric Mitchell, Zanele Munyikwa, Suraj Nair, Avanika Narayan, Deepak Narayanan, Ben Newman, Allen Nie, Juan Carlos Niebles, Hamed Nilforoshan, Julian Nyarko, Giray Ogut, Laurel Orr, Isabel Papadimitriou, Joon Sung Park, Chris Piech, Eva Portelance, Christopher Potts, Aditi Raghunathan, Rob Reich, Hongyu Ren, Frieda Rong, Yusuf Roohani, Camilo Ruiz, Jack Ryan, Christopher Ré, Dorsa Sadigh, Shiori Sagawa, Keshav Santhanam, Andy Shih, Krishnan Srinivasan, Alex Tamkin, Rohan Taori, Armin W. Thomas, Florian Tramèr, Rose E. Wang, William Wang, Bohan Wu, Jiajun Wu, Yuhuai Wu, Sang Michael Xie, Michihiro Yasunaga, Jiaxuan You, Matei Zaharia, Michael Zhang, Tianyi Zhang, Xikun Zhang, Yuhui Zhang, Lucia Zheng, Kaitlyn Zhou, and Percy Liang. 2021. On the opportunities and risks of foundation models.

Kenneth Ward Church, Zeyu Chen, and Yanjun Ma. 2021a. Emerging trends: A gentle introduction to fine-tuning. *Natural Language Engineering*, 27(6):763–778.

Kenneth Ward Church and Valia Kordoni. 2022. Emerging trends: Sota-chasing. *Natural Language Engineering*, 28(2):249–269.

Kenneth Ward Church, Xiaopeng Yuan, Sheng Guo, Zewu Wu, Yehua Yang, and Zeyu Chen. 2021b. Emerging trends: Deep nets for poets. *Natural Language Engineering*, 27(5):631–645.

Robert Dale. 2021. Gpt-3: What's it good for? *Natural Language Engineering*, 27(1):113–118.

Ernest Davis. 2013. Qualitative spatial reasoning in interpreting text and narrative. *Spatial Cognition & Computation*, 13(4):264–294.

Ernest Davis and Gary Marcus. 2015. Commonsense reasoning and commonsense knowledge in artificial intelligence. *Communications of the ACM*, 58(9):92–103.

Jacob Devlin, Ming-Wei Chang, Kenton Lee, and Kristina Toutanova. 2019. BERT: Pre-training of deep bidirectional transformers for language understanding. In *Proceedings of the 2019 Conference of the North American Chapter of the Association for Computational Linguistics: Human Language Technologies, Volume 1 (Long and Short Papers)*, pages 4171–4186, Minneapolis, Minnesota. Association for Computational Linguistics.

Esin Durmus, He He, and Mona Diab. 2020. FEQA: A question answering evaluation framework for faithfulness assessment in abstractive summarization. In *Proceedings of the 58th Annual Meeting of the Association for Computational Linguistics*, pages 5055–5070, Online. Association for Computational Linguistics.

Allyson Ettinger. 2020. What BERT is not: Lessons from a new suite of psycholinguistic diagnostics for language models. *Transactions of the Association for Computational Linguistics*, 8:34–48.

John R Firth. 1957. A synopsis of linguistic theory, 1930-1955. *Studies in linguistic analysis*.

Andrew S Gordon and Jerry R Hobbs. 2017. *A formal theory of commonsense psychology: How people think people think*. Cambridge University Press.

Herbert P Grice. 1975. Logic and conversation. In P. Cole and J. Morgan, editors, *Syntax and Semantices: Vol 3: Speech Acts*. Academic Press, London.

Zellig S Harris. 1954. Distributional structure. *Word*, 10(2-3):146–162.

Dirk Hovy and Shrimai Prabhumoye. 2021. Five sources of bias in natural language processing. *Language and Linguistics Compass*, 15(8):e12432.

Jeremy Howard and Sebastian Ruder. 2018. Universal language model fine-tuning for text classification. In *Proceedings of the 56th Annual Meeting of the Association for Computational Linguistics (Volume 1: Long Papers)*, pages 328–339, Melbourne, Australia. Association for Computational Linguistics.

Henry A Kautz, James F Allen, et al. 1986. Generalized plan recognition. In *AAAI*, volume 86, page 5.

Diane J Litman and James F Allen. 1987. A plan recognition model for subdialogues in conversations. *Cognitive science*, 11(2):163–200.

Gary Marcus and Ernest Davis. 2019. *Rebooting AI: Building artificial intelligence we can trust.* Pantheon Press.

Cade Metz. 2020. When A.I. falls in love. *The New York Times*. Nov. 24, 2020.

Anne-Laure Rousseau and Clément Baudelaire. 2020. Doctor GPT-3: Hype or reality? *Nabla*.

Alex Wang, Amanpreet Singh, Julian Michael, Felix Hill, Omer Levy, and Samuel Bowman. 2018. GLUE: A multi-task benchmark and analysis platform for natural language understanding. In *Proceedings of the 2018 EMNLP Workshop BlackboxNLP: Analyzing and Interpreting Neural Networks for NLP*, pages 353–355, Brussels, Belgium. Association for Computational Linguistics.

Zhihan Zhang, Xiubo Geng, Tao Qin, Yunfang Wu, and Daxin Jiang. 2021. Knowledge-aware procedural text understanding with multi-stage training. In *Proceedings of the Web Conference 2021*, pages 3512–3523.

ACL Tutorial Proposal: Towards Reproducible Machine Learning Research in Natural Language Processing

Ana Lucic[1], Maurits Bleeker[1], Samarth Bhargav[1], Jessica Zosa Forde[2], Koustuv Sinha[3], Jesse Dodge[4], Sasha Luccioni[5] and Robert Stojnic[6]

[1]University of Amsterdam
[2]Brown University
[3]McGill University
[4]Allen Institute of AI
[5]HuggingFace
[6]Meta AI

1 Motivation & Objectives

While recent progress in the field of ML has been significant, the reproducibility of these cutting-edge results is often lacking, with many submissions lacking the necessary information in order to ensure subsequent reproducibility (Hutson, 2018). Despite proposals such as the Reproducibility Checklist (Pineau et al., 2020) and reproducibility criteria at several major conferences (NAACL, 2021; Dodge, 2020a; Beygelzimer et al., 2021), the reflex for carrying out research with reproducibility in mind is lacking in the broader ML community. We propose this tutorial as a gentle introduction to ensuring reproducible research in ML, with a specific emphasis on computational linguistics and NLP.

2 Target Audience and Prerequisites

This tutorial targets senior researchers in academic institutions who want to include reproducibility initiatives in their coursework, and well as junior researchers who are interested in participating in reproducibility initiatives. The only prerequisite for this tutorial is a basic understanding of the scientific method.

3 Outline of Tutorial Content

The tutorial will cover four parts over the course of three hours:

1. Introduction to reproducibility (45 mins)
2. Reproducibility in NLP (45 mins)
3. Mechanisms for Reproducibility (45 mins)
4. Reproducibility as a Teaching Tool (45 mins)

3.1 Introduction to reproducibility (45 mins)

We will start the tutorial by motivating the overall problem: what does reproducibility mean and why is it important? What does it mean for research results to (not) be reproducible? What are some examples of important results that were (not) reproducible? Why is there a reproducibility crisis in ML (Hutson, 2018)? What would it look like if we, as a community, prioritized reproducibility?

We will explain how reproducibility works in fields outside of computer science, such as medicine or psychology, explain the mechanisms they use, and the criteria for achieving reproducible results. Next, we will discusses successes and failures of reproducibility in these fields, the reasons why the research was (not) reproducible, and the resulting consequences. We will follow with a similar discussion of fields within computer science, specifically in ML, before diving into reproducibility in NLP.

3.2 Reproducibility in NLP (45 mins)

In this part of the tutorial, we will focus on reproducibility in NLP, including examples of results that were reproducible and those that were not reproducible. For the latter, we will categorize reproducibility failures in NLP. We will also discuss the specific challenges with reproducibility in NLP and how they differ from the challenges in ML, and in science more broadly.

3.3 Mechanisms for Reproducibility (45 mins)

After explaining what reproducibility is and what the challenges are, we will examine existing mechanisms for reproducibility in ML and NLP, such as reproducibility checklists (Pineau et al., 2020; NAACL, 2021; Dodge, 2020a; Beygelzimer et al.,

Proceedings of the 60th Annual Meeting of the Association for Computational Linguistics: Tutorial Abstracts, pages 7 - 11
May 22-27, 2022 ©2022 Association for Computational Linguistics

2021), ACM's badging system (ACM, 2019), and reproducibility tracks at conferences (ECIR, 2021). We will follow with an in-depth discussion on the ML Reproducibility Challenge[1], where the objective is to investigate the results of papers at top ML conferences by reproducing the experiments. Finally, we will discuss in length on useful tips, methodologies and tools researchers and practitioners in NLP can use to enforce and encourage reproducibility in their own work.

3.4 Reproducibility as a Teaching Tool (45 mins)

To improve the scientific process, scientific discourse, and science in general, it is imperative that we teach the next generation of academics and researchers about conducting reproducible research. In the final part of the tutorial, we will provide recommendations for using reproducibility as a teaching tool based on our experiences with incorporating a reproducibility project into a graduate-level course (Lucic et al., 2021; Lucic, 2021; Dodge, 2020b). We will share our experiences and reflect on the lessons learned, with the goal of providing instructors with a playbook for implementing a reproducibility project in a computer science course. Next to that, we will also give an overview of how reproducibility has been used as a tool in other academic courses.

4 Breadth of the tutorial

In the tutorial, we introduce and contrast reproducibility (Drummond, 2009), discuss papers reflecting on the reproducibility crisis in ML and NLP (Pedersen, 2008; Mieskes et al., 2019; Belz et al., 2021a,b), including possible reasons for this crisis (Hutson, 2018). This includes barriers to reproducibility, such as lack of code availability (Pedersen, 2008; Wieling et al., 2018) and the influence of different experimental setups (Fokkens et al., 2013; Bouthillier et al., 2019; Picard, 2021).

Raff (2019) investigates the reproducibility of ML papers without accessing provided code, relying on only details provided in the paper. (Belz, 2021) attempt to quantify reproducibility in NLP and ML. We also discuss reproducibility checklists from multiple venues (Pineau et al., 2020; NAACL, 2021; Dodge, 2020a; Beygelzimer et al., 2021; ACM, 2019; ECIR, 2021). Finally, we discuss coursework focused on teaching through reproducibility in ML (Yildiz et al., 2021) and FACT-AI (Lucic et al., 2021; Lucic, 2021).

5 Reading List

We briefly describe recommended reading for participants in this section.

5.1 General Background

Heaven (2020) (link) provides an overview of the replicability/reproducibility crisis in AI, noting common barriers, potential solutions and their drawbacks. Interested readers can also refer to (Baker, 2016) for a general discussion of the replicability/reproducibility crises in science.

5.2 NLP

We recommend participants read the following papers about reproducibility in NLP: (Mieskes et al., 2019; Belz et al., 2021a).

5.3 Teaching Reproducibility

Yildiz et al. (2021) introduce a portal[2], focusing on teaching AI/ML through 'low-barrier' reproducibility projects. They show that this can help develop critical thinking skills w.r.t. research, and that participants placed more value on scientific reproductions.

6 Sharing of Tutorial Materials

All of our tutorial materials will be publicly available at `https://acl-reproducibility-tutorial.github.io`.

7 Ethics Statement

Reproducibility and ethics are inherently related, since ensuring that research is reproducible by members of the community that are not its original authors contributes to making the field more inclusive (e.g. providing the code and hyperparameters needed to replicated a state-of-the-art ML model can help researchers build and expand upon it). Furthermore, being transparent about the costs of the model, both in terms of the computational power need to train it as well as the data involved, helps members of the community be more equitable in evaluating it: for instance, if two models achieved similar accuracy on the same dataset, with one requiring 10x more computation than the other,

[1] `https://paperswithcode.com/rc2021`

[2] `https://reproducedpapers.org/`

that could help researchers choose which one to use given their constraints. Finally, progress in the field of computational linguistics specifically is being led by large organizations that are the ones training and deploying equally large language models that are difficult to replicate without having access to the same resources that they do; being more transparent and ensuring that even large language models are replicable is important for making the field more democratic as a whole.

8 Pedagogical Material

As mentioned in Section 3.4, we want instructors to be able to use content from our tutorial in order to design reproducibility projects for graduate-level coursework. The content will largely be based on the following components: (i) a blog post on how to use the ML Reproducibility Challenge as an educational tool (Dodge, 2020b), (ii) blog post on one university's experience in using the ML Reproducibility Challenge as an educational tool (Lucic, 2021), and (iii) the corresponding paper (Lucic et al., 2021). We hope this can function as a starter pack for any instructor who is interesting in incorporating reproducibility projects in their coursework.

9 Presenter Information

Ana Lucic is a PhD Candidate at the University of Amsterdam. Her work primarily focuses on developing and evaluating methods for explainable machine learning (ML). She co-developed a graduate-level course called *Fairness, Accountability, Confidentiality and Transparency in Artificial Intelligence (FACT-AI)* that is centered around reproducing existing FACT-AI algorithms. Her email is `a.lucic@uva.nl`.

Maurits Bleeker is PhD Candidate at the University of Amsterdam who co-developed the FACT-AI course. His main interest lies in the development of new optimization functions for image-text matching, by taking task- and data-specific inductive priors into account. This with the goal to improve the computational efficiency of multi-modal optimization. He also co-developed and coordinated two iterations of the FACT-AI course at the University of Amsterdam. His email is `m.j.r.bleeker@uva.nl`.

Samarth Bhargav is a PhD Candidate at the University of Amsterdam. Samarth's research focuses on representation learning for information retrieval, with a goal of making IR systems (e.g recommenders) more amenable to user control, for example, through conversational interfaces. His secondary interests include recommendation in a cross-market or cross-domain setting, known-item retrieval, FACT in IR and teaching IR. He has co-developed and taught multiple iterations of graduate IR courses at the University of Amsterdam. His email is `s.bhargav@uva.nl`.

Jessica Zosa Forde is a PhD Candidate at Brown University. Jessica's research focuses on the empirical study of deep learning models, to improve their reliability in high stakes domains such as healthcare. She has also studied the inductive bias of overparameterized models, and model pruning. She believes that the open science movement is important for improving transparency and accountability in ML. She is also am a co-organizer of the ML Reproducibility Challenge (MLRC) and the ML Retrospectives workshop. Her email is `jessica_forde@brown.edu`.

Koustuv Sinha is a PhD Candidate at McGill University/Mila. He is the lead organizer of the annual ML Reproducibility Challenge (MLRC), which has had five iterations since 2018 (at ICLR 2018, ICLR 2019, NeurIPS 2019, MLRC 2020, MLRC 2021). He also serves as an associate editor of ReScience, a journal promoting reproducibility reports in various fields of science. Koustuv's research focuses on investigating systematicity in natural language understanding (NLU) models, especially the state-of-the-art large language models. His research goal is to develop methods to analyze the failure cases in robustness and systematicity of these NLU models, and develop methods to alleviate them in production. His email is `koustuv.sinha@mail.mcgill.ca`.

Jesse Dodge is a research Scientist at AllenNLP, Allen Institute for AI. Jesse created the NLP Reproducibility Checklist, has been an organizer of the ML Reproducibility Challenge (MLRC) 2020 and 2021, will be a Reproducibility Chair at NAACL 2022, and has published numerous papers in top NLP conferences on reproducibility. Jesse's research focuses on efficient and reproducible NLP and ML. He also has experience building large-scale NLP datasets. His email is `jessed@allenai.org`.

Sasha Luccioni is a Research Scientist at HuggingFace. She has been an organizer of the ML Reproducibility Challenge (MLRC) since 2021 and is an Area Chair for the Ethics in NLP track at EMNLP 2021. Sasha's research aims to contribute towards understanding the data and techniques used for developing Machine Learning approaches. She is particularly interested in developing tools for analyzing and filtering the data used for training large language models, as well as quantifying their carbon footprint. She has lectured several classes in ML and NLP, and is the main instructor for the forthcoming Deeplearning AI "AI for Social Good" course. Her email is `sasha.luccioni@huggingface.co`.

Robert Stojnic an Engineering Manager at Meta AI (formerly Facebook AI Research). He is the co-creator of Papers with Code, which has the biggest collection of papers, code, datasets and associated results, and co-organizes the ML Reproducibility Challenge (MLRC). He created the ML Code Completeness Checklist (Stojnic, 2020), which is part of the ML Reproducibility Checklist used by multiple conferences, including NeurIPS. He is a co-organizator for ML Reproducibility Challenge. His email is `rstojnic@fb.com`.

References

ACM. 2019. Artifact review and badging. https://www.acm.org/publications/policies/artifact-review-badging.

Monya Baker. 2016. 1,500 scientists lift the lid on reproducibility. *Nature News*, 533(7604):452.

Anya Belz. 2021. Quantifying reproducibility in nlp and ml. *arXiv preprint arXiv:2109.01211*.

Anya Belz, Shubham Agarwal, Anastasia Shimorina, and Ehud Reiter. 2021a. A systematic review of reproducibility research in natural language processing. In *Proceedings of the 16th Conference of the European Chapter of the Association for Computational Linguistics: Main Volume*, pages 381–393, Online. Association for Computational Linguistics.

Anya Belz, Anastasia Shimorina, Shubham Agarwal, and Ehud Reiter. 2021b. The ReproGen shared task on reproducibility of human evaluations in NLG: Overview and results. In *Proceedings of the 14th International Conference on Natural Language Generation*, pages 249–258, Aberdeen, Scotland, UK. Association for Computational Linguistics.

Alina Beygelzimer, Yann Dauphin, Percy Liang, and Jennifer Wortman-Vaughan. 2021. Introducing the neurips 2021 paper checklist. https://neuripsconf.medium.com/introducing-the-neurips-2021-paper-checklist.

Xavier Bouthillier, César Laurent, and Pascal Vincent. 2019. Unreproducible research is reproducible. In *International Conference on Machine Learning*, pages 725–734. PMLR.

Jesse Dodge. 2020a. Guest post: Reproducibility at emnlp 2020. https://2020.emnlp.org/blog/2020-05-20-reproducibility.

Jesse Dodge. 2020b. The reproducibility challenge as an educational tool. Medium, https://medium.com/paperswithcode/the-reproducibility-challenge-as-an-educational-tool-cd1596e3716c.

Chris Drummond. 2009. Replicability is not reproducibility: nor is it good science.

ECIR. 2021. Ecir: Call for reproducibility track papers. https://www.ecir2021.eu/call-for-reproducibility-track.

Antske Fokkens, Marieke van Erp, Marten Postma, Ted Pedersen, Piek Vossen, and Nuno Freire. 2013. Offspring from reproduction problems: What replication failure teaches us. In *Proceedings of the 51st Annual Meeting of the Association for Computational Linguistics (Volume 1: Long Papers)*, pages 1691–1701, Sofia, Bulgaria. Association for Computational Linguistics.

Will Douglas Heaven. 2020. Ai is wrestling with a replication crisis.

Matthew Hutson. 2018. Artificial intelligence faces reproducibility crisis. *Science*, 359:725–726.

Ana Lucic. 2021. Case study: How your course can incorporate the reproducibility challenge. Medium, https://medium.com/paperswithcode/case-study-how-your-course-can-incorporate-the-reproducibility-challenge-76e260a2b59.

Ana Lucic, Maurits Bleeker, Sami Jullien, Samarth Bhargav, and Maarten de Rijke. 2021. Teaching fairness, accountability, confidentiality, and transparency in artificial intelligence through the lens of reproducibility.

Margot Mieskes, Karën Fort, Aurélie Névéol, Cyril Grouin, and Kevin Cohen. 2019. Community perspective on replicability in natural language processing. In *Proceedings of the International Conference on Recent Advances in Natural Language Processing (RANLP 2019)*, pages 768–775, Varna, Bulgaria. INCOMA Ltd.

MLRC. Machine learning reproducibility challenge 2021. https://paperswithcode.com/rc2021.

NAACL. 2021. Naacl 2021 reproducibility checklist. https://2021.naacl.org/calls/reproducibility-checklist/.

Ted Pedersen. 2008. Last words: Empiricism is not a matter of faith. *Computational Linguistics*, 34(3):465–470.

David Picard. 2021. Torch. manual_seed (3407) is all you need: On the influence of random seeds in deep learning architectures for computer vision. *arXiv preprint arXiv:2109.08203*.

Joelle Pineau, Philippe Vincent-Lamarre, Koustuv Sinha, Vincent Lariviere, Alina Beygelzimer, Florence d'Alche Buc, Emily Fox, and Hugo Larochelle. 2020. Improving reproducibility in machine learning research (a report from the neurips 2019 reproducibility program). *Journal of Machine Learning Research*.

Edward Raff. 2019. A step toward quantifying independently reproducible machine learning research. *Advances in Neural Information Processing Systems*, 32:5485–5495.

Robert Stojnic. 2020. Ml code completeness checklist. Medium, https://medium.com/paperswithcode/ml-code-completeness-checklist-e9127b168501.

Martijn Wieling, Josine Rawee, and Gertjan van Noord. 2018. Squib: Reproducibility in computational linguistics: Are we willing to share? *Computational Linguistics*, 44(4):641–649.

Burak Yildiz, Hayley Hung, Jesse H Krijthe, Cynthia CS Liem, Marco Loog, Gosia Migut, Frans A Oliehoek, Annibale Panichella, Przemysław Pawełczak, Stjepan Picek, et al. 2021. Reproducedpapers. org: Openly teaching and structuring machine learning reproducibility. In *International Workshop on Reproducible Research in Pattern Recognition*, pages 3–11. Springer.

Knowledge-Augmented Methods for Natural Language Processing

Chenguang Zhu[1], Yichong Xu[1], Xiang Ren[2], Bill Yuchen Lin[2], Meng Jiang[3], Wenhao Yu[3]
[1]Microsoft Cognitive Services Research, [2]University of Southern California,
[3]University of Notre Dame
{chezhu, yicxu}@microsoft.com, {xiangren, yuchen.lin}@usc.edu,
{mjiang2, wyu1}@nd.edu

1 Information

Keywords Knowledge-augmented Methods, Commonsense Reasoning, Natural Language Understanding, Natural Language Generation.

Tutorial description Knowledge in NLP has been a rising trend especially after the advent of large-scale pre-trained models. Knowledge is critical to equip statistics-based models with common sense, logic and other external information. In this tutorial, we will introduce recent state-of-the-art works in applying knowledge in language understanding, language generation and commonsense reasoning.

Suggested duration Half day (3 hours)

Type of Tutorial Cutting-edge

Targeted Audience Target audience are researchers and practitioners in natural language processing, knowledge graph and common sense reasoning. The audience will learn about the state-of-the-art research in integrating knowledge into NLP to improve the cognition capability of models.

Outline

- Introduction to NLP and Knowledge (15 min)
- Knowledge in Natural Language Understanding (55 min)
- Knowledge in Natural Language Generation (55 min)
- Commonsense Knowledge and Reasoning for NLP (55 min)

Similar tutorials There have been several tutorials/workshops on knowledge in NLP:

- Tutorial at AAAI 2021: Commonsense Knowledge Acquisition and Representation
- Tutorial at EMNLP 2021: Knowledge-Enriched Natural Language Generation
- KR2ML workshop at NeurIPS 2019 and 2020: Knowledge Representation & Reasoning Meets Machine Learning
- Tutorial at ACL 2020: Commonsense Reasoning for Natural Language Processing

Diversity considerations The use of knowledge is not limited to any specific language. The technologies we introduce are generally applicable to all languages, as long as there is corresponding corpus and knowledge sources, e.g., dictionaries, knowledge graph, etc. We have a diverse instructor team across multiple institutions (i.e., MS, USC, UND). The team has a diverse and broad expertise in natural language processing and generation, machine learning, and various application domains.

2 Brief Tutorial Outline

In recent years, the field of natural language processing has considerably benefited from larger-scale models, better training strategies, and greater availability of data, exemplified by BERT* (Devlin et al., 2019), RoBERTa* (Liu et al., 2019b), and GPT models (Radford et al., 2018, 2019; Brown et al., 2020). It has been shown that these pre-trained language models can effectively characterize linguistic patterns in text and generate high-quality context-aware representations (Liu et al., 2019a). However, these models are trained in a way where the only input is the source text. As a result, these models struggle to grasp external world knowledge about concepts, relations, and common sense (Poerner et al., 2019; Talmor et al., 2020).

In this tutorial, we use *Knowledge* to refer to this external information which is absent from model input yet useful for the model to produce target output. Knowledge is important for language representation and should be included into the training and inference of language models. Knowledge is also an indispensable component to enable higher levels of intelligence which is unattainable from statistical learning on input text patterns.

2.1 Knowledge-augmented Natural Language Understanding

In natural language understanding (NLU), the task is to make predictions about the property of words, phrases, sentences or paragraphs based on the input text, e.g., sentiment analysis, named entity recognition and language inference. We will introduce how to use knowledge to augment NLU models

Proceedings of the 60th Annual Meeting of the Association for Computational Linguistics: Tutorial Abstracts, pages 12 - 20

along the dimension of knowledge source: i) structured knowledge such as knowledge graph, and ii) unstructured knowledge such as text corpus.

We first discuss efforts to integrate structured knowledge into language understanding, which can be categorized into explicit methods via concept/entity embeddings (Zhang et al., 2019; Peters et al., 2019; Liu et al., 2020; Yu et al., 2020a; Zeng et al., 2020) and implicit methods via entity masking prediction (Sun et al., 2019; Shen et al., 2020; Xiong et al., 2020; Wang et al., 2019). For example, ERNIE* (Zhang et al., 2019) explicitly pre-trains the entity embeddings on a knowledge graph using TransE (Bordes et al., 2013), while EAE (Févry et al., 2020) learns the representation as model parameters. KEPLER (Wang et al., 2019) implicitly calculates entity embeddings using a pre-trained language model based on the description text. Recently, some works propose to co-train the knowledge graph module and the language model (Ding et al., 2019; Lv et al., 2020; Yu et al., 2022b). For example, JAKET* (Yu et al., 2022b) proposes to use the knowledge module to produce embeddings for entities in text while using the language module to generate context-aware initial embeddings for entities and relations in the knowledge graph. Yu et al. (2022c) and Xu et al. (2021)* propose to use dictionary descriptions as additional knowledge source for natural language understanding and commonsense reasoning tasks.

We then introduce how to integrate unstructured knowledge into NLU models. This usually requires a text retrieval module to obtain related text from knowledge corpus. There have been multiple approaches to adopt unstructured knowledge, especially for open-domain QA task. For example, Lee et al. (2019) first trains a retriever by inverse cloze task (ICT) and then jointly trains the retriever and reader for open-domain QA. DPR* (Karpukhin et al., 2020) conducts supervised training for the retriever and achieves better performance on open-domain QA. REALM (Guu et al., 2020) predicts masked salient spans consisting of entities to jointly pre-train the reader and retriever. KG-FiD (Yu et al., 2022a) proposed to filter noisy passages by leveraging the structural relationship among the retrieved passages with a knowledge graph during retrieval.

We will introduce the above methods and focus on three key aspects of employing knowledge in NLU tasks: i) how to ground the input into knowledge domain (e.g., entity linking), ii) how to represent knowledge (e.g., graph neural network), and iii) how to integrate knowledge information into the NLU models (e.g., attention).

2.2 Knowledge-augmented Natural Language Generation

The goal of natural language generation (NLG) is to produce understandable text in human language from linguistic or non-linguistic data in a variety of forms such as textual data, image data, and structured knowledge graph (Yu et al., 2020b). Different from natural language understanding (NLU) methods, NLG methods are typically under the encoder-decoder generation framework (Sutskever et al., 2014; Bahdanau et al., 2015), which poses unique challenges for leveraging knowledge into decoding the next tokens during generation.

We will first present the existing methods for integrating knowledge into NLG models. These models are categorized into three major paradigms which incorporate knowledge through (1) *model architectures* that facilitate the use of knowledge, such as knowledge-related attention mechanism, knowledge-related copy/pointer mechanisms (Zhou et al., 2018; Zhang et al., 2020a; Liu et al., 2021a; Guan et al., 2020a; Dong et al., 2021); (2) *learning frameworks* that inject knowledge information into the generation models through training, such as posterior regularization, constraint-driven learning, semantic loss, knowledge-informed weak supervision (Hu et al., 2016, 2018; Tan et al., 2020; Dinan et al., 2019); (3) *inference methods* which imposes on the inference process different knowledge constraints to guide decoding, such as lexical constraints, task-specific objectives, global inter-dependency (Dathathri et al., 2020; Qin et al., 2020).

In addition to presenting the unified model architectures/frameworks, we will introduce several specific methods based on different knowledge sources. The knowledge sources can be divided into structured knowledge such as knowledge graph, or unstructured such as text corpus. Many methods have been proposed to learn the relationship between structured knowledge and input/output sequences. They can be categorized into four methodologies: injecting pre-computed knowledge embeddings into language generation (Zhou et al., 2018); transferring knowledge into language model with triplet information (Guan et al., 2020a); performing reasoning over knowledge graph via path finding strategies (Liu et al., 2019c; Ji et al., 2020a; Yu et al., 2022d); and improve the graph embeddings with graph neural networks (Zhang et al., 2020a; Ji et al., 2020b). For example, Zhou et al. (2018) enriched the context representations of the input sequence with neighbouring concepts on ConceptNet using graph attention. Recently, some work attempted to integrate external commonsense knowledge into generative pretrained language models (Guan et al., 2020a; Bhagavatula et al., 2020). For example, Guan et al. (2020a) conducted post-training on synthetic data constructed from commonsense KG by translating triplets into natural language texts.

To handle different kinds of relationships between unstructured text and input/output sequences, existing methods can be categorized into two methodologies: guiding generation with retrieved information (Ghazvininejad et al., 2018; Lewis et al., 2020; Wang et al., 2021); modeling background knowledge into text generation (Qin et al., 2019; Meng et al., 2020; Zeng et al., 2021). For example, Lewis et al. (2020) introduced a general retrieval-augmented generation (RAG) framework by leveraging a pre-trained neural retriever and generator. It can be easily fine-tuned on downstream tasks, and it has demonstrated state-of-the-art performance on various knowledge-intensive natural language generation tasks.

2.3 Commonsense Knowledge and Reasoning for Natural Language Processing

Humans reason and make decisions in everyday settings by using *common sense*, which consists of basic knowledge (*e.g.*, regarding the physical world or human social behavior) that is rarely taught explicitly yet shared by almost everyone. Commonsense knowledge and the ability of using common sense to reason is thus of vital significance for developing human-like NLP models as well as general-purpose AI systems. We will cover topics as follows: (1) **resources** and **datasets** for developing and benchmarking commonsense reasoning methods. (2) **knowledge-aware commonsense reasoning methods** for both understanding and generation tasks. (3) **analysis** on the acquired commonsense knowledge of pre-trained LMs and the behavior of knowledge-augmented commonsense reasoning methods.

There is a recent surge of novel knowledge resources and the benchmark datasets for researching commonsense in the NLP domain. One of the most widely used commonsense knowledge resource is ConceptNet (Speer et al., 2017), which is a binary, relational knowledge graph. Although ConceptNet enjoys simplicity and popularity, its incompleteness and concept-centric structures limit the development of more general topics on commonsense reasoning for NLP. We present the recent works on developing commonsense knowledge resources, such as ASER (Zhang et al., 2021), AscentKB (Nguyen et al., 2021), COMET-ATOMIC2020 (Hwang et al., 2021), and GenericsKB (Bhakthavatsalam et al., 2020), which provide us with event-centric, large-scale, neural-symbolic, semi-structured ways to access and model commonsense knowledge. We then introduce the popular datasets for evaluating the commonsense reasoning methods that span three main categories: 1) multiple-choice QA (e.g., CommonsenseQA (Talmor et al., 2019), SocialIQA (Sap et al., 2019), PhysicalIQA (Bisk et al., 2020), RiddleSense (Lin et al., 2021b)), 2) open-ended QA (e.g., ProtoQA (Boratko et al., 2020) OpenCSR (Lin et al., 2021a)), 3) constrained NLG (e.g., CommonGen (Lin et al., 2020b), conversation generation).

To equip language models (LMs) with commonsense reasoning ability, researchers have developed many knowledge-augmented reasoning models that fit different task formulations. For the multiple-choice QA setting, we introduce a set of knowledge-augmented neuro-symbolic methods: KagNet* (Lin et al., 2019), HyKAS (Ma et al., 2019), MHGRN* (Feng et al., 2020), HybridGN (Yan et al., 2020) and QA-GNN* (Yasunaga et al., 2021). These methods make use of structured knowledge graphs and/or neural commonsense KBs for injecting external knowledge structures to neural LMs. As for the open-ended setting, we present the DrKIT (Dhingra et al., 2020) and DrFact* (Lin et al., 2021a) reasoning frameworks, which are both designed for differentiable reasoning over a virtual knowledge graph (i.e., an un/semi-structured text corpus).

For generation-based commonsense tasks, we present knowledge-augmented text generation models that are designed for generative commonsense: 1) EKI-BART (Fan et al., 2020), KG-BART* (Liu et al., 2021b), and RE-T5* (Wang et al., 2021) for the CommonGen task, 2) commonsense knowledge-enhanced story generation models (Guan et al., 2019, 2020b), and 3) commonsense-based models for conversation generation, such as ConceptFlow* (Zhang et al., 2020b) and CARE (Zhong et al., 2021).

Apart from the benchmarking and modeling, we also introduce the analysis works that aim to provide a deeper understanding the commonsense knowledge of pre-trained LMs: LAMA Probing* (Petroni et al., 2019), NumerSense (Lin et al., 2020a), and RICA* (Zhou et al., 2020). In addition, we also introduce the line of works that focus on interpreting the reasoning mechanism of the knowledge-augmented reasoning methods (Raman et al., 2021; Chan et al., 2021; Rajani et al., 2019).

2.4 Short Reading List

- Knowledge-augmented NLU: (Zhang et al., 2019; Peters et al., 2019; Liu et al., 2020; Ding et al., 2019; Lv et al., 2020; Yu et al., 2022b);
- Knowledge-augmented NLG: (Zhou et al., 2018; Zhang et al., 2020a; Ji et al., 2020b; Lewis et al., 2020; Wang et al., 2021);
- Commonsense Knowledge and Reasoning for NLP: (Lin et al., 2019; Ma et al., 2019; Fan et al., 2020; Liu et al., 2021b; Wang et al., 2021; Guan et al., 2019, 2020b).
- Relevant Survey: (Yu et al., 2020b; Yang et al., 2021; Zhang et al., 2022; Wei et al., 2021)

3 Presenters

Chenguang Zhu is a Principal Research Manager in Microsoft Cognitive Services Research Group, where he leads the Knowledge & Language Team. His research in NLP covers knowledge graph, text summarization and task-oriented dialogue. Dr. Zhu has led teams to achieve first places in multiple NLP competitions, including CommonsenseQA, CommonGen, FEVER, CoQA, ARC and SQuAD v1.0. He holds a Ph.D. degree in Computer Science from Stanford University. Dr. Zhu has given talks at Stanford University, Carnegie Mellon University and University of Notre Dame. He has previously been TA for Coursera online class "Automata", giving teaching sessions to 100K international students. Additional information is available at `https://www.microsoft.com/en-us/research/people/chezhu/`.

Yichong Xu is a Senior Researcher in Knowledge & Language Team in Microsoft Cognitive Services Research Group. His research in NLP focuses on using external knowledge to help natural language processing, including question answering, commonsense reasoning, and text summarization. Dr. Xu received his Ph.D. in Machine Learning from Carnegie Mellon University. During his time at CMU, he has been TA for large classes ($>$ 200 students) on machine learning and convex optimization. Dr. Xu has given talks at CMU AI Seminar, as well as in many international conferences including ACL, NAACL, NeurIPS, ICML, etc. Additional information is available at `https://xycking.wixsite.com/yichongxu`.

Xiang Ren is an assistant professor at the USC Computer Science Department, a Research Team Leader at USC ISI, and the PI of the Intelligence and Knowledge Discovery (INK) Lab at USC. Priorly, he received his Ph.D. in Computer Science from the University of Illinois Urbana-Champaign. Dr. Ren works on knowledge acquisition and reasoning in natural language processing, with focuses on developing human-centered and label-efficient computational methods for building trustworthy NLP systems. Ren publishes over 100 research papers and delivered over 10 tutorials at the top conferences in natural language process, data mining, and artificial intelligence. He received NSF CAREER Award, The Web Conference Best Paper runner-up, ACM SIGKDD Doctoral Dissertation Award, and several research awards from Google, Amazon, JP Morgan, Sony, and Snapchat. He was named Forbes' Asia 30 Under 30 in 2019. Additional information is available at `https://shanzhenren.github.io/`.

Bill Yuchen Lin is a Ph.D. candidate at USC. His research goal is to teach machines to think, talk, and act with commonsense knowledge and commonsense reasoning ability as humans do. Towards this ultimate goal, he has been developing knowledge-augmented reasoning methods (e.g., KagNet, MHGRN, DrFact) and constructing benchmark datasets (e.g., CommonGen, RiddleSense, X-CSR) that require commonsense knowledge and complex reasoning for both NLU and NLG. He initiated an online compendium of commonsense reasoning research, which serves as a portal site for the community. More information is available at `https://yuchenlin.xyz/`.

Meng Jiang is an assistant professor at the Department of Computer Science and Engineering in the University of Notre Dame. He obtained his bachelor degree and PhD from Tsinghua University. His research interests include data mining, machine learning, and natural language processing. He has published more than 100 peer-reviewed papers of these topics. He is the recipient of Notre Dame International Faculty Research Award. The honors and awards he received include best paper finalist in KDD 2014, best paper award in KDD-DLG workshop 2020, and ACM SIGSOFT Distinguished Paper Award in ICSE 2021. He received NSF CRII award in 2019 and CAREER award in 2022. Additional information is available at `http://www.meng-jiang.com/`.

Wenhao Yu is a Ph.D. student in the Department of Computer Science and Engineering at the University of Notre Dame. His research lies in controllable knowledge-driven natural language processing, particularly in natural language generation. His research has been published in top-ranked NLP and data mining conferences such as ACL, EMNLP, KDD and WWW. Additional information is available at `https://wyu97.github.io/`.

Acknowledgements

Xiang Ren and Bill Yuchen Lin are supported in part by the Office of the Director of National Intelligence (ODNI), Intelligence Advanced Research Projects Activity (IARPA), via Contract No. 2019-19051600007, the DARPA MCS program under Contract No. N660011924033, the Defense Advanced Research Projects Agency with award W911NF-19-20271, NSF IIS 2048211, NSF SMA 1829268, and gift awards from Google, Amazon, JP Morgan and Sony. Wenhao Yu and Meng Jiang are supported in part by the National Science Foundation (NSF) grants IIS-1849816, CCF-1901059, IIS-2119531 and IIS-2142827, and gift awards from Amazon and Snap research.

References

Dzmitry Bahdanau, Kyunghyun Cho, and Yoshua Bengio. 2015. Neural machine translation by jointly learning to align and translate. In *3rd International Conference on Learning Representations, 2015*.

Chandra Bhagavatula, Ronan Le Bras, Chaitanya Malaviya, Keisuke Sakaguchi, Ari Holtzman, Hannah Rashkin, Doug Downey, Wen-tau Yih, and Yejin Choi. 2020. Abductive commonsense reasoning. In *8th International Conference on Learning Representations, ICLR 2020*. OpenReview.net.

Sumithra Bhakthavatsalam, Chloe Anastasiades, and P. Clark. 2020. Genericskb: A knowledge base of generic statements. *ArXiv*, abs/2005.00660.

Yonatan Bisk, Rowan Zellers, Ronan LeBras, Jianfeng Gao, and Yejin Choi. 2020. PIQA: reasoning about physical commonsense in natural language. In *The Thirty-Fourth AAAI Conference on Artificial Intelligence, AAAI 2020*.

Michael Boratko, Xiang Li, Tim O'Gorman, Rajarshi Das, Dan Le, and Andrew McCallum. 2020. ProtoQA: A question answering dataset for prototypical common-sense reasoning. In *Proceedings of the 2020 Conference on Empirical Methods in Natural Language Processing (EMNLP)*, Online.

Antoine Bordes, Nicolas Usunier, Alberto García-Durán, Jason Weston, and Oksana Yakhnenko. 2013. Translating embeddings for modeling multi-relational data. In *Advances in Neural Information Processing Systems*, pages 2787–2795.

Tom B. Brown, Benjamin Mann, Nick Ryder, Melanie Subbiah, Jared Kaplan, Prafulla Dhariwal, Arvind Neelakantan, Pranav Shyam, Girish Sastry, Amanda Askell, Sandhini Agarwal, Ariel Herbert-Voss, Gretchen Krueger, Tom Henighan, Rewon Child, Aditya Ramesh, Daniel M. Ziegler, Jeffrey Wu, Clemens Winter, Christopher Hesse, Mark Chen, Eric Sigler, Mateusz Litwin, Scott Gray, Benjamin Chess, Jack Clark, Christopher Berner, Sam McCandlish, Alec Radford, Ilya Sutskever, and Dario Amodei. 2020. Language models are few-shot learners. In *Advances in Neural Information Processing Systems*.

Aaron Chan, Soumya Sanyal, Bo Long, Jiashu Xu, Tanishq Gupta, and Xiang Ren. 2021. Salkg: Learning from knowledge graph explanations for commonsense reasoning. *ArXiv*, abs/2104.08793.

Sumanth Dathathri, Andrea Madotto, Janice Lan, Jane Hung, Eric Frank, Piero Molino, Jason Yosinski, and Rosanne Liu. 2020. Plug and play language models: A simple approach to controlled text generation. In *8th International Conference on Learning Representations, ICLR 2020*.

Jacob Devlin, Ming-Wei Chang, Kenton Lee, and Kristina Toutanova. 2019. BERT: Pre-training of deep bidirectional transformers for language understanding. In *Proceedings of the 2019 Conference of the North American Chapter of the Association for Computational Linguistics: Human Language Technologies*, Minneapolis, Minnesota.

Bhuwan Dhingra, Manzil Zaheer, Vidhisha Balachandran, Graham Neubig, Ruslan Salakhutdinov, and William W. Cohen. 2020. Differentiable reasoning over a virtual knowledge base. In *8th International Conference on Learning Representations, ICLR 2020*.

Emily Dinan, Stephen Roller, Kurt Shuster, Angela Fan, Michael Auli, and Jason Weston. 2019. Wizard of wikipedia: Knowledge-powered conversational agents. In *7th International Conference on Learning Representations, ICLR 2019*.

Ming Ding, Chang Zhou, Qibin Chen, Hongxia Yang, and Jie Tang. 2019. Cognitive graph for multi-hop reading comprehension at scale. In *Proceedings of the 57th Annual Meeting of the Association for Computational Linguistics*, Florence, Italy.

Xiangyu Dong, Wenhao Yu, Chenguang Zhu, and Meng Jiang. 2021. Injecting entity types into entity-guided text generation. In *Conference on Empirical Methods in Natural Language Processing (EMNLP)*.

Zhihao Fan, Yeyun Gong, Zhongyu Wei, Siyuan Wang, Yameng Huang, Jian Jiao, Xuanjing Huang, Nan Duan, and Ruofei Zhang. 2020. An enhanced knowledge injection model for commonsense generation. In *Proceedings of the 28th International Conference on Computational Linguistics*, Barcelona, Spain (Online).

Yanlin Feng, Xinyue Chen, Bill Yuchen Lin, Peifeng Wang, Jun Yan, and Xiang Ren. 2020. Scalable multi-hop relational reasoning for knowledge-aware question answering. In *Proceedings of the 2020 Conference on Empirical Methods in Natural Language Processing (EMNLP)*, pages 1295–1309, Online. Association for Computational Linguistics.

Thibault Févry, Livio Baldini Soares, Nicholas FitzGerald, Eunsol Choi, and Tom Kwiatkowski. 2020. Entities as experts: Sparse memory access with entity supervision. In *Proceedings of the 2020 Conference on Empirical Methods in Natural Language Processing (EMNLP)*, Online.

Marjan Ghazvininejad, Chris Brockett, Ming-Wei Chang, Bill Dolan, Jianfeng Gao, Wen-tau Yih, and Michel Galley. 2018. A knowledge-grounded neural conversation model. In *Proceedings of the Thirty-Second AAAI Conference on Artificial Intelligence, (AAAI-18)*, pages 5110–5117. AAAI Press.

Jian Guan, Fei Huang, Zhihao Zhao, Xiaoyan Zhu, and Minlie Huang. 2020a. A knowledge-enhanced pretraining model for commonsense story generation. *Transactions of the Association for Computational Linguistics*, 8:93–108.

Jian Guan, Fei Huang, Zhihao Zhao, Xiaoyan Zhu, and Minlie Huang. 2020b. A knowledge-enhanced pretraining model for commonsense story generation. *Transactions of the Association for Computational Linguistics*, 8:93–108.

Jian Guan, Yansen Wang, and Minlie Huang. 2019. Story ending generation with incremental encoding and commonsense knowledge. In *The Thirty-Third AAAI Conference on Artificial Intelligence, AAAI 2019*, pages 6473–6480. AAAI Press.

Kelvin Guu, Kenton Lee, Zora Tung, Panupong Pasupat, and Ming-Wei Chang. 2020. Realm: Retrieval-augmented language model pre-training. *arXiv preprint arXiv:2002.08909*.

Zhiting Hu, Xuezhe Ma, Zhengzhong Liu, Eduard Hovy, and Eric Xing. 2016. Harnessing deep neural networks with logic rules. In *Proceedings of the 54th Annual Meeting of the Association for Computational Linguistics (Volume 1: Long Papers)*, pages 2410–2420, Berlin, Germany. Association for Computational Linguistics.

Zhiting Hu, Zichao Yang, Ruslan Salakhutdinov, Lianhui Qin, Xiaodan Liang, Haoye Dong, and Eric P. Xing. 2018. Deep generative models with learnable knowledge constraints. In *Advances in Neural Information Processing Systems 31: Annual Conference on Neural Information Processing Systems 2018, NeurIPS 2018, December 3-8, 2018, Montréal, Canada*, pages 10522–10533.

Jena D. Hwang, Chandra Bhagavatula, Ronan Le Bras, Jeff Da, Keisuke Sakaguchi, Antoine Bosselut, and Yejin Choi. 2021. Comet-atomic 2020: On symbolic and neural commonsense knowledge graphs. In *AAAI*.

Haozhe Ji, Pei Ke, Shaohan Huang, Furu Wei, and Minlie Huang. 2020a. Generating commonsense explanation by extracting bridge concepts from reasoning paths. In *Conference of the Asia-Pacific Chapter of the Association for Computational Linguistics and International Joint Conference on Natural Language (AACL-IJCNLP)*.

Haozhe Ji, Pei Ke, Shaohan Huang, Furu Wei, Xiaoyan Zhu, and Minlie Huang. 2020b. Language generation with multi-hop reasoning on commonsense knowledge graph. In *Proceedings of the 2020 Conference on Empirical Methods in Natural Language Processing (EMNLP)*, pages 725–736, Online. Association for Computational Linguistics.

Vladimir Karpukhin, Barlas Oguz, Sewon Min, Patrick Lewis, Ledell Wu, Sergey Edunov, Danqi Chen, and Wen-tau Yih. 2020. Dense passage retrieval for open-domain question answering. In *Proceedings of the 2020 Conference on Empirical Methods in Natural Language Processing (EMNLP)*, Online.

Kenton Lee, Ming-Wei Chang, and Kristina Toutanova. 2019. Latent retrieval for weakly supervised open domain question answering. In *Proceedings of the 57th Annual Meeting of the Association for Computational Linguistics*, pages 6086–6096, Florence, Italy. Association for Computational Linguistics.

Patrick S. H. Lewis, Ethan Perez, Aleksandra Piktus, Fabio Petroni, Vladimir Karpukhin, Naman Goyal, Heinrich Küttler, Mike Lewis, Wen-tau Yih, Tim Rocktäschel, Sebastian Riedel, and Douwe Kiela. 2020. Retrieval-augmented generation for knowledge-intensive NLP tasks. In *Advances in Neural Information Processing Systems 33: Annual Conference on Neural Information Processing Systems 2020, NeurIPS 2020, December 6-12, 2020, virtual*.

Bill Yuchen Lin, Xinyue Chen, Jamin Chen, and Xiang Ren. 2019. KagNet: Knowledge-aware graph networks for commonsense reasoning. In *Proceedings of the 2019 Conference on Empirical Methods in Natural Language Processing and the 9th International Joint Conference on Natural Language Processing (EMNLP-IJCNLP)*, pages 2829–2839, Hong Kong, China. Association for Computational Linguistics.

Bill Yuchen Lin, Seyeon Lee, Rahul Khanna, and Xiang Ren. 2020a. Birds have four legs?! NumerSense: Probing Numerical Commonsense Knowledge of Pre-Trained Language Models. In *Proceedings of the 2020 Conference on Empirical Methods in Natural Language Processing (EMNLP)*, pages 6862–6868, Online. Association for Computational Linguistics.

Bill Yuchen Lin, Haitian Sun, Bhuwan Dhingra, Manzil Zaheer, Xiang Ren, and William Cohen. 2021a. Differentiable open-ended commonsense reasoning. In *Proceedings of the 2021 Conference of the North American Chapter of the Association for Computational Linguistics: Human Language Technologies*, pages 4611–4625, Online. Association for Computational Linguistics.

Bill Yuchen Lin, Ziyi Wu, Yichi Yang, Dong-Ho Lee, and Xiang Ren. 2021b. Riddlesense: Reasoning about riddle questions featuring linguistic creativity and commonsense knowledge. In *ACL*.

Bill Yuchen Lin, Wangchunshu Zhou, Ming Shen, Pei Zhou, Chandra Bhagavatula, Yejin Choi, and Xiang Ren. 2020b. CommonGen: A constrained text generation challenge for generative commonsense reasoning. In *Findings of the Association for Computational Linguistics: EMNLP 2020*, pages 1823–1840, Online. Association for Computational Linguistics.

Nelson F. Liu, Matt Gardner, Yonatan Belinkov, Matthew E. Peters, and Noah A. Smith. 2019a. Linguistic knowledge and transferability of contextual representations. In *Proceedings of the 2019 Conference of the North American Chapter of the Association for Computational Linguistics: Human Language Technologies, Volume 1 (Long and Short Papers)*, pages 1073–1094, Minneapolis, Minnesota. Association for Computational Linguistics.

Weijie Liu, Peng Zhou, Zhe Zhao, Zhiruo Wang, Qi Ju, Haotang Deng, and Ping Wang. 2020. K-BERT: enabling language representation with knowledge graph. In *The Thirty-Fourth AAAI Conference on Artificial Intelligence, AAAI 2020, The Thirty-Second Innovative Applications of Artificial Intelligence Conference, IAAI 2020, The Tenth AAAI Symposium on Educational Advances in Artificial Intelligence, EAAI 2020, New York, NY, USA, February 7-12, 2020*, pages 2901–2908. AAAI Press.

Ye Liu, Yao Wan, Lifang He, Hao Peng, and Philip S Yu. 2021a. Kg-bart: Knowledge graph-augmented bart for generative commonsense reasoning. In *AAAI Conference on Artificial Intelligence (AAAI)*.

Ye Liu, Yao Wan, Lifang He, Hao Peng, and Philip S. Yu. 2021b. Kg-bart: Knowledge graph-augmented bart for generative commonsense reasoning. In *AAAI*.

Yinhan Liu, Myle Ott, Naman Goyal, Jingfei Du, Mandar Joshi, Danqi Chen, Omer Levy, Mike Lewis, Luke Zettlemoyer, and Veselin Stoyanov. 2019b. Roberta: A robustly optimized bert pretraining approach. *arXiv preprint arXiv:1907.11692*.

Zhibin Liu, Zheng-Yu Niu, Hua Wu, and Haifeng Wang. 2019c. Knowledge aware conversation generation with reasoning on augmented graph. In *Conference on Empirical Methods in Natural Language Processing and International Joint Conference on Natural Language Processing (EMNLP-IJCNLP)*.

Shangwen Lv, Daya Guo, Jingjing Xu, Duyu Tang, Nan Duan, Ming Gong, Linjun Shou, Daxin Jiang, Guihong Cao, and Songlin Hu. 2020. Graph-based reasoning over heterogeneous external knowledge for commonsense question answering. In *The Thirty-Fourth AAAI Conference on Artificial Intelligence, AAAI 2020*, pages 8449–8456. AAAI Press.

Kaixin Ma, Jonathan Francis, Quanyang Lu, Eric Nyberg, and Alessandro Oltramari. 2019. Towards generalizable neuro-symbolic systems for commonsense question answering. In *Proceedings of the First Workshop on Commonsense Inference in Natural Language Processing*, pages 22–32, Hong Kong, China. Association for Computational Linguistics.

Chuan Meng, Pengjie Ren, Zhumin Chen, Christof Monz, Jun Ma, and Maarten de Rijke. 2020. Refnet: A reference-aware network for background based conversation. In *AAAI Conference on Artificial Intelligence (AAAI)*.

Tuan-Phong Nguyen, Simon Razniewski, and G. Weikum. 2021. Advanced semantics for commonsense knowledge extraction. *Proceedings of the Web Conference 2021*.

Matthew E. Peters, Mark Neumann, Robert Logan, Roy Schwartz, Vidur Joshi, Sameer Singh, and Noah A. Smith. 2019. Knowledge enhanced contextual word representations. In *Proceedings of the 2019 Conference on Empirical Methods in Natural Language Processing and the 9th International Joint Conference on Natural Language Processing (EMNLP-IJCNLP)*, pages 43–54, Hong Kong, China. Association for Computational Linguistics.

Fabio Petroni, Tim Rocktäschel, Sebastian Riedel, Patrick Lewis, Anton Bakhtin, Yuxiang Wu, and Alexander Miller. 2019. Language models as knowledge bases? In *Proceedings of the 2019 Conference on Empirical Methods in Natural Language Processing and the 9th International Joint Conference on Natural Language Processing (EMNLP-IJCNLP)*, pages 2463–2473, Hong Kong, China. Association for Computational Linguistics.

Nina Poerner, Ulli Waltinger, and Hinrich Schütze. 2019. Bert is not a knowledge base (yet): Factual knowledge vs. name-based reasoning in unsupervised qa. *arXiv preprint arXiv:1911.03681*.

Lianhui Qin, Michel Galley, Chris Brockett, Xiaodong Liu, Xiang Gao, Bill Dolan, Yejin Choi, and Jianfeng Gao. 2019. Conversing by reading: Contentful neural conversation with on-demand machine reading. In *Annual Meeting of the Association for Computational Linguistics (ACL)*.

Lianhui Qin, Vered Shwartz, Peter West, Chandra Bhagavatula, Jena D Hwang, Ronan Le Bras, Antoine Bosselut, and Yejin Choi. 2020. Backpropagation-based decoding for unsupervised counterfactual and abductive reasoning. In *Proceedings of the 2020 Conference on Empirical Methods in Natural Language Processing (EMNLP)*, pages 794–805.

Alec Radford, Karthik Narasimhan, Tim Salimans, and Ilya Sutskever. 2018. Improving language understanding by generative pre-training.

Alec Radford, Jeffrey Wu, Rewon Child, David Luan, Dario Amodei, and Ilya Sutskever. 2019. Language models are unsupervised multitask learners. *OpenAI Blog*, 1(8):9.

Nazneen Fatema Rajani, Bryan McCann, Caiming Xiong, and Richard Socher. 2019. Explain yourself! leveraging language models for commonsense reasoning. In *Proceedings of the 57th Annual Meeting of the Association for Computational Linguistics*, Florence, Italy.

Mrigank Raman, Siddhant Agarwal, Peifeng Wang, Aaron Chan, Hansen Wang, Sungchul Kim, Ryan A. Rossi, Handong Zhao, Nedim Lipka, and Xiang Ren. 2021. Learning to deceive knowledge graph augmented models via targeted perturbation. *ArXiv*, abs/2010.12872.

Maarten Sap, Hannah Rashkin, Derek Chen, Ronan Le Bras, and Yejin Choi. 2019. Social IQa: Commonsense reasoning about social interactions. In *Proceedings of the 2019 Conference on Empirical Methods in Natural Language Processing and the 9th International Joint Conference on Natural Language Processing (EMNLP-IJCNLP)*, pages 4463–4473, Hong Kong, China. Association for Computational Linguistics.

Tao Shen, Yi Mao, Pengcheng He, Guodong Long, Adam Trischler, and Weizhu Chen. 2020. Exploiting structured knowledge in text via graph-guided representation learning. In *Proceedings of the 2020 Conference on Empirical Methods in Natural Language Processing (EMNLP)*, pages 8980–8994, Online. Association for Computational Linguistics.

Robyn Speer, Joshua Chin, and Catherine Havasi. 2017. Conceptnet 5.5: An open multilingual graph of general knowledge. In *Proceedings of the Thirty-First AAAI Conference on Artificial Intelligence*.

Yu Sun, Shuohuan Wang, Yukun Li, Shikun Feng, Xuyi Chen, Han Zhang, Xin Tian, Danxiang Zhu, Hao Tian, and Hua Wu. 2019. Ernie: Enhanced representation through knowledge integration. *arXiv preprint arXiv:1904.09223*.

Ilya Sutskever, Oriol Vinyals, and Quoc V. Le. 2014. Sequence to sequence learning with neural networks. In *Advances in Neural Information Processing Systems 27: Annual Conference on Neural Information Processing Systems 2014, December 8-13 2014, Montreal, Quebec, Canada*, pages 3104–3112.

Alon Talmor, Yanai Elazar, Yoav Goldberg, and Jonathan Berant. 2020. oLMpics-on what language model pre-training captures. *Transactions of the Association for Computational Linguistics*, 8:743–758.

Alon Talmor, Jonathan Herzig, Nicholas Lourie, and Jonathan Berant. 2019. CommonsenseQA: A question answering challenge targeting commonsense knowledge. In *Proceedings of the 2019 Conference of the North American Chapter of the Association for Computational Linguistics: Human Language Technologies, Volume 1 (Long and Short Papers)*, pages 4149–4158, Minneapolis, Minnesota. Association for Computational Linguistics.

Bowen Tan, Lianhui Qin, Eric Xing, and Zhiting Hu. 2020. Summarizing text on any aspects: A knowledge-informed weakly-supervised approach. In *Proceedings of the 2020 Conference on Empirical Methods in Natural Language Processing (EMNLP)*, pages 6301–6309, Online. Association for Computational Linguistics.

Han Wang, Yang Liu, Chenguang Zhu, Linjun Shou, Ming Gong Gong, Yichong Xu, and Michael Zeng. 2021. Retrieval enhanced model for commonsense generation. In *Annual Meeting of Association for Computational Linguistics (ACL)*.

Xiaozhi Wang, Tianyu Gao, Zhaocheng Zhu, Zhiyuan Liu, Juanzi Li, and Jian Tang. 2019. Kepler: A unified model for knowledge embedding and pretrained language representation. *arXiv preprint arXiv:1911.06136*.

Xiaokai Wei, Shen Wang, Dejiao Zhang, Parminder Bhatia, and Andrew Arnold. 2021. Knowledge enhanced pretrained language models: A compreshensive survey. *arXiv preprint arXiv:2110.08455*.

Wenhan Xiong, Jingfei Du, William Yang Wang, and Veselin Stoyanov. 2020. Pretrained encyclopedia: Weakly supervised knowledge-pretrained language model. In *8th International Conference on Learning Representations, ICLR 2020, Addis Ababa, Ethiopia, April 26-30, 2020*. OpenReview.net.

Yichong Xu, Chenguang Zhu, Ruochen Xu, Yang Liu, Michael Zeng, and Xuedong Huang. 2021. Fusing context into knowledge graph for commonsense reasoning. In *ACL*.

Jun Yan, Mrigank Raman, Tianyu Zhang, Ryan A. Rossi, Handong Zhao, Sungchul Kim, Nedim Lipka, and Xiang Ren. 2020. Learning contextualized knowledge structures for commonsense reasoning. *ArXiv*, abs/2010.12873.

Jian Yang, Gang Xiao, Yulong Shen, Wei Jiang, Xinyu Hu, Ying Zhang, and Jinghui Peng. 2021. A survey of knowledge enhanced pre-trained models. *arXiv preprint arXiv:2110.00269*.

Michihiro Yasunaga, Hongyu Ren, Antoine Bosselut, Percy Liang, and Jure Leskovec. 2021. QA-GNN: Reasoning with language models and knowledge graphs for question answering. In *Proceedings of the 2021 Conference of the North American Chapter of the Association for Computational Linguistics: Human Language Technologies*, pages 535–546, Online. Association for Computational Linguistics.

Donghan Yu, Chenguang Zhu, Yuwei Fang, Wenhao Yu, Shuohang Wang, Yichong Xu, Xiang Ren, Yiming Yang, and Michael Zeng. 2022a. Kg-fid: Infusing knowledge graph in fusion-in-decoder for open-domain question answering. *Annual Meeting of the Association for Computational Linguistics (ACL)*.

Donghan Yu, Chenguang Zhu, Yiming Yang, and Michael Zeng. 2022b. Jaket: Joint pre-training of knowledge graph and language understanding. *AAAI Conference on Artificial Intelligence (AAAI)*.

Wenhao Yu, Mengxia Yu, Tong Zhao, and Meng Jiang. 2020a. Identifying referential intention with heterogeneous contexts. In *Proceedings of The Web Conference 2020*.

Wenhao Yu, Chenguang Zhu, Yuwei Fang, Donghan Yu, Shuohang Wang, Yichong Xu, Michael Zeng, and Meng Jiang. 2022c. Dict-bert: Enhancing language model pre-training with dictionary. *Annual Meeting of the Association for Computational Linguistics (ACL).*

Wenhao Yu, Chenguang Zhu, Zaitang Li, Zhiting Hu, Qingyun Wang, Heng Ji, and Meng Jiang. 2020b. A survey of knowledge-enhanced text generation. *ACM Computing Survey (CSUR).*

Wenhao Yu, Chenguang Zhu, Lianhui Qin, Zhihan Zhang, Tong Zhao, and Meng Jiang. 2022d. Diversifying content generation for commonsense reasoning with mixture of knowledge graph experts. In *Annual Meeting of the Association for Computational Linguistics (ACL).*

Qingkai Zeng, Jinfeng Lin, Wenhao Yu, Jane Cleland-Huang, and Meng Jiang. 2021. Enhancing taxonomy completion with concept generation via fusing relational representations. In *ACM SIGKDD International Conference on Knowledge Discovery & Data Mining (KDD).*

Qingkai Zeng, Wenhao Yu, Mengxia Yu, Tianwen Jiang, Tim Weninger, and Meng Jiang. 2020. Tri-train: Automatic pre-fine tuning between pre-training and fine-tuning for sciner. In *Findings of the Association for Computational Linguistics: EMNLP 2020*, pages 4778–4787.

Hongming Zhang, Xin Liu, Haojie Pan, Hao Ke, Jiefu Ou, Tianqing Fang, and Yangqiu Song. 2021. Aser: Towards large-scale commonsense knowledge acquisition via higher-order selectional preference over eventualities. *ArXiv.*

Houyu Zhang, Zhenghao Liu, Chenyan Xiong, and Zhiyuan Liu. 2020a. Grounded conversation generation as guided traverses in commonsense knowledge graphs. In *Proceedings of the 58th Annual Meeting of the Association for Computational Linguistics*, pages 2031–2043, Online. Association for Computational Linguistics.

Houyu Zhang, Zhenghao Liu, Chenyan Xiong, and Zhiyuan Liu. 2020b. Grounded conversation generation as guided traverses in commonsense knowledge graphs. In *Proceedings of the 58th Annual Meeting of the Association for Computational Linguistics*, Online.

Zhengyan Zhang, Xu Han, Zhiyuan Liu, Xin Jiang, Maosong Sun, and Qun Liu. 2019. ERNIE: Enhanced language representation with informative entities. In *Proceedings of the 57th Annual Meeting of the Association for Computational Linguistics*, pages 1441–1451, Florence, Italy. Association for Computational Linguistics.

Zhihan Zhang, Wenhao Yu, Mengxia Yu, Zhichun Guo, and Meng Jiang. 2022. A survey of multi-task learning in natural language processing: Regarding task relatedness and training methods. *arXiv preprint arXiv:2204.03508.*

Peixiang Zhong, Di Wang, Pengfei Li, Chen Zhang, Hao Wang, and C. Miao. 2021. Care: Commonsense-aware emotional response generation with latent concepts. In *AAAI.*

Hao Zhou, Tom Young, Minlie Huang, Haizhou Zhao, Jingfang Xu, and Xiaoyan Zhu. 2018. Commonsense knowledge aware conversation generation with graph attention. In *Proceedings of the Twenty-Seventh International Joint Conference on Artificial Intelligence, IJCAI 2018, July 13-19, 2018, Stockholm, Sweden*, pages 4623–4629. ijcai.org.

Pei Zhou, Rahul Khanna, Seyeon Lee, Bill Yuchen Lin, Daniel Ho, Jay Pujara, and Xiang Ren. 2020. Rica: Evaluating robust inference capabilities based on commonsense axioms. *arXiv: Computation and Language.*

Non-Autoregressive Sequence Generation

Jiatao Gu
Facebook AI Research
jgu@fb.com

Xu Tan
Microsoft Research Asia
xuta@microsoft.com

1 Tutorial Description

State-of-the-art sequence generation models are mostly autoregressive (AR, Vaswani et al., 2017; Brown et al., 2020) where each generation step depends on the previously generated tokens. However, such models are inherently sequential, leading to high latency at inference time and suffering label bias (Lafferty et al., 2001) problem due to the locally normalized searching steps and exposure bias (Bengio et al., 2015) problem due to mismatch between training and inference.

Recently, increasing attention has been paid to modeling sequence generation in a non- or semi-autoregressive manner, which attempts to generate the entire or partial output sequences in parallel to speed up the decoding process and avoid potential issues (e.g., label bias, exposure bias) in autoregressive generation. In this tutorial, for simplicity, we summarize both approaches as *non-autoregressive* (NAR) sequence generation models. NAR models have been explored in many sequence generation tasks for text (e.g., neural machine translation (Gu et al., 2018), text summarization (Gu et al., 2019), text error correction (Awasthi et al., 2019; Leng et al., 2021b)), speech (e.g., speech recognition (Chen et al., 2019) and speech synthesis (Ren et al., 2019)). However, naive NAR models still face many challenges to close the performance gap between state-of-the-art autoregressive models because of a lack of modeling power. This tutorial will provide a thorough introduction and review of the basics of non-autoregressive sequence generation, including the background, the capabilities, and limits, popular methods that improve NAR models, and their applications on text and speech generation.

Introduction The tutorial will start with a brief discussion on the motivation of NAR generation, the problem definition, the evaluation protocol, and the comparison with standard autoregressive approaches. We use machine translation as the example generation task for the in-depth discussion as the first of its kind in NLP (Gu et al., 2018), and many follow-ups focus on this direction. Notably, we will show the underlying reasons (i.e., multimodality problem) why NAR models generally perform worse and give some high-level instructions on improving NAR systems (Gu et al., 2018; Ren et al., 2020; Gu and Kong, 2021).

Methods Based on the high-level instructions, we will then dive into the detailed improvements from five aspects: *model architecture*, *objective function*, *training data*, *learning paradigm*, and *additional inference tricks*, respectively.

For *model architecture*, we divide existing approaches into four major categories according to the inference process: (1) **fully NAR models** that outputs the whole sequence in a single forward pass (Gu et al., 2018; Kaiser et al., 2018; Guo et al., 2019; Gu and Kong, 2021); (2) **iteration-based NAR models** which iteratively refine the parallel decoding results (Lee et al., 2018; Ghazvininejad et al., 2019, 2020b; Gu et al., 2019; Kasai et al., 2020); (3) **partially NAR models** where a sequence is still predicted autoregressively while each step multiple tokens are generated in parallel (Wang et al., 2018; Stern et al., 2018, 2019; Deng and Rush, 2020); (4) **locally AR models** which are, on the other hand, overall NAR while predict "phrases" autoregressively (Huang et al., 2017; Kong et al., 2020b). Aside from these major types, explicitly modeling NAR with **latent variables** is another useful approach that can boost the overall capability of all above NAR models. We will highlight several implementations including latent fertilities (Gu et al., 2018) and alignments (Saharia et al., 2020), VAEs with continuous (Shu et al., 2020; Lee et al., 2020; Gu and Kong, 2021) or discrete (Kaiser et al., 2018; Roy et al., 2018) latent variables, flow-based models (Ma et al., 2019b)

Proceedings of the 60th Annual Meeting of the Association for Computational Linguistics: Tutorial Abstracts, pages 21 - 27
May 22-27, 2022

and stochastic diffusion models.

Next, we will discuss in-depth the *objective function* of NAR models starting from the standard cross-entropy (CE) loss which, however, leads to duplicated tokens in NAR outputs. To overcome this, we will introduce two types of advanced objective functions in this tutorial: (1) **loss function with latent information** which can be effectively marginalized/approximated through dynamic programming. For instance, we will cover latent alignments (CTC, AXE) (Graves et al., 2006; Libovický and Helcl, 2018; Saharia et al., 2020; Ghazvininejad et al., 2020a) and latent orders (OAXE) (Du et al., 2021); (2) the other type of objective function focuses on **loss beyond token-level**, which considers n-gram (Shao et al., 2020; Liu et al., 2021) or sequence-level (Sun et al., 2019; Shao et al., 2019; Tu et al., 2020) energy to optimize NAR models.

From the perspective of *training data*, we will first describe the sequence-level knowledge distillation (KD, Kim and Rush, 2016), and then explain its effectiveness of using KD on NAR generation (Zhou et al., 2020; Xu et al., 2021). In addition, we will also include the discussion about the drawbacks of over-relying on distillation for training NAR models (Ding et al., 2020) and propose potential alternatives.

For the fourth part, we will deepen the discussion on how to train NAR models more effectively. Due to the lack of modeling power, it may be crucial for NAR models to be trained with a more suitable *learning paradigm* to help match the performance of AR systems. In this tutorial, we will introduce the previous efforts from three primary directions: (1) **curriculum learning** where we train NAR models with tasks from easy to difficult progressively (Guo et al., 2020a; Liu et al., 2020; Qian et al., 2020); (2) **adversarial training** where a discriminator is jointly learned and the NAR model is forced to fool the discriminator. In this way, NAR models will not be directly exposed to the real training data, which is "too difficult" to fit. Adversarial training itself is not so popular in text generation in general. However, it is widely applied in other modalities such as NAR speech synthesis (Kong et al., 2020a). (3) **pre-training** where we will also show that combining with recent advances in self-supervised pre-training (e.g., BERT), we can naturally leverage the monolingual data to improve the learning of NAR models (Guo et al., 2020b; Qi et al., 2021; Jiang et al., 2021).

At the end of this part, we will also include additional discussions on valuable methods and tricks which help NAR models at inference time. For example, searching with length beams, reranking the AR model, incorporating the n-gram language model, etc.

Applications In the third section, we review some typical tasks that adopt non-autoregressive sequence generation, including *text generation* and *speech generation*. For *text generation*, we cover several tasks: (1) **neural machine translation** (Gu et al., 2018; Lee et al., 2018; Wang et al., 2018; Kong et al., 2020b; Gu and Kong, 2021); (2) **text summarization** (Gu et al., 2019; Qi et al., 2021; Jiang et al., 2021); (3) **text error correction** (Awasthi et al., 2019; Mallinson et al., 2020; Leng et al., 2021a,b); (4) **automatic speech recognition** (Chen et al., 2019; Higuchi et al., 2020; Chan et al., 2020). For *speech generation*, we cover: (1) **text to speech** (Ren et al., 2019; Peng et al., 2020; Oord et al., 2018; Kim et al., 2020, 2021); (2) **voice conversion** (Hayashi et al., 2021; Kameoka et al., 2021).

Beyond the introduction of task-level characteristics for non-autoregressive sequence generation, we also introduce some *advanced topics in applications*, including: (1) some advanced length prediction methods for text summarization (Qi et al., 2021) and speech recognition (Chen et al., 2019); (2) alignment modeling between source and target sequence in text to speech, e.g., duration prediction (Ren et al., 2019) or source-target attention (Peng et al., 2020); (3) analysis on the dependency among target tokens that can influence the modeling difficulty of non-autoregressive generation models (Ren et al., 2020); (4) the relationship between non-autoregressive sequence generation and streaming sequence generation (Ma et al., 2019a), considering they are both for inference speedup.

Conclusion At the end of the tutorial, we will describe several research challenges and list the comparison with other speed-up approaches for AR models (e.g., quantization, pruning, distillation). Finally, we will also discuss the potential future research directions to close this tutorial.

2 Type of the Tutorial

Cutting-edge.

3 Target Audience

This tutorial targets those audiences who work on 1) neural sequence generation (e.g., neural machine translation, etc.); 2) natural language and speech processing; 3) deep learning and artificial intelligence in general. Some prerequisites for the attendees are:

- Math: calculus, linear algebra, and probability theory.
- Machine learning: basic machine learning paradigms and basic deep learning models such as MLP, RNN, CNN, and Transformer.
- Neural sequence generation: Be familiar with at least one sequence generation task, such as neural machine translation, text summarization, automatic speech recognition, text to speech, etc.

4 Tutorial Outline

PART I Introduction ($\sim$ 20 minutes)

- 1.1 Problem definition
- 1.2 Evaluation protocol
- 1.3 Multi-modality problem

PART II Methods ($\sim$ 90 minutes)

- 2.1 Model architectures
  - 2.1.1 Fully NAR models
  - 2.1.2 Iteration-based NAR models
  - 2.1.3 Partially NAR models
  - 2.1.4 Locally AR models
  - 2.1.5 NAR models with latent variables
- 2.2 Objective functions
  - 2.2.1 Loss with latent variables
  - 2.2.2 Loss beyond token-level
- 2.3 Training data
- 2.4 Learning paradigms
  - 2.4.1 Curriculum learning
  - 2.4.2 Adversarial training
  - 2.4.3 Self-supervised pre-training
- 2.5 Inference methods and tricks

PART III Applications ($\sim$ 50 minutes)

- 3.1 Text generation
  - 3.1.1 Neural machine translation
  - 3.1.2 Text summarization
  - 3.1.3 Text error correction
  - 3.1.4 Automatic speech recognition
- 3.2 Speech generation
  - 3.2.1 Text to speech
  - 3.2.2 Voice conversion
- 3.3 Advanced topics in applications
  - 3.3.1 Advanced length prediction
  - 3.3.2 Alignment (duration vs attention)
  - 3.3.3 Target token dependency
  - 3.3.4 Relationship with streaming

PART IV Open problems, future directions, Q&A ($\sim$20 minutes)

5 How the tutorial includes other people's work

We organize our tutorial content from a broad view of non-autoregressive sequence generation, spanning from basic methods to applications, which cover diverse work in this area, most of which are other people's work.

6 Diversity Considerations

Methods We introduce the methods of non-autoregressive sequence generation in a comprehensive and diverse view, covering model architectures, objective functions, training data, learning paradigms, and additional tricks. These methods are general and not limited to specific languages or domains.

Applications We introduce a variety of non-autoregressive sequence generation tasks, spanning from the text (e.g., neural machine translation, text error correction) to speech (e.g., text to speech, voice conversion).

Instructors We are from different institutions (Facebook and Microsoft) and work on diverse topics in machine learning, NLP, and non-autoregressive sequence generation.

Audiences Due to the diversity in the methods and applications of our tutorial and the tutorial instructors, we can attract audiences interested in diverse sequence generation tasks and modalities (text and speech) and from both academia and industry.

7 Reading List

Please see the citations in Section 1. For participants interested in reading important studies before this tutorial, we recommend the following basic papers: (1) the typical AR model (Transformer) (Vaswani et al., 2017); (2) the vanilla NAR model (Gu et al., 2018); (3) the typical iteration-based NAR model (Ghazvininejad et al., 2019); (4) a study on NAR models for both text and speech tasks (Ren et al., 2020).

8 Bio of Speakers

8.1 Jiatao Gu

Dr. Jiatao Gu is a Research Scientist at Facebook AI Research (FAIR). Jiatao received his Ph.D. degree in 2018 from the University of Hong Kong and B.Eng from Tsinghua University in 2014. His research interests cover representation learning and generative models and their applications on NLP, speech, computer vision, and multi-modal learning. Particularly, his research focuses on developing efficient learning and inference algorithms and applying them successfully to neural machine translation and 3D-aware image synthesis. He has over 40 papers published at top-tier conferences and journals, including ACL, EMNLP, NeurIPS, ICLR, and TACL. Jiao has also served as an area chair for several top conferences. Jiatao has rich research experience on the topic of non-autoregressive sequence generation. He published the first of its kind paper for non-autoregressive neural machine translation in 2018 and has led the following exploration and extensions. Website: `https://jiataogu.me/`.

8.2 Xu Tan

Xu Tan is a Senior Researcher at Microsoft Research Asia (MSRA). His research interests cover deep learning and its applications in language/speech/music, including neural machine translation, text to speech, automatic speech recognition, pre-training, music generation, etc. The machine translation systems have achieved human parity on Chinese-English news translation in 2018 and won several champions on WMT machine translation competition in 2019. He has designed several popular language/speech/music models, and systems (e.g., MASS, FastSpeech, and Muzic) and has transferred many research works to the products in Microsoft (e.g., Azure, Bing). He has rich research experiences on non-autoregressive sequence generation and has designed several models such as FastCorrect 1/2, FastSpeech 1/2. He has given several tutorials on language/speech/music at international conferences: 1) A tutorial on text to speech at IJCAI 2021; 2) A tutorial on AI music composition at ACM Multimedia 2021. Website: `https://www.microsoft.com/en-us/research/people/xuta/`.

9 Ethics Statement

Non-autoregressive sequence generation can improve the inference speed of various sequence generation tasks in text and speech. Unfortunately, this technology may be misused to generate deepfake content (Thies et al., 2016) such as mimicking one's writing style or speaking style. However, great attempts have been made to detect the deepfake content (Kaggle, 2019), which can minimize or avoid its potential negative impact.

References

Abhijeet Awasthi, Sunita Sarawagi, Rasna Goyal, Sabyasachi Ghosh, and Vihari Piratla. 2019. Parallel iterative edit models for local sequence transduction. In *Proceedings of the 2019 Conference on Empirical Methods in Natural Language Processing and the 9th International Joint Conference on Natural Language Processing (EMNLP-IJCNLP)*, pages 4259–4269, Hong Kong, China. Association for Computational Linguistics.

Samy Bengio, Oriol Vinyals, Navdeep Jaitly, and Noam Shazeer. 2015. Scheduled sampling for sequence prediction with recurrent neural networks. In *NIPS*, pages 1171–1179.

Tom B Brown, Benjamin Mann, Nick Ryder, Melanie Subbiah, Jared Kaplan, Prafulla Dhariwal, Arvind Neelakantan, Pranav Shyam, Girish Sastry, Amanda Askell, et al. 2020. Language models are few-shot learners. *arXiv preprint arXiv:2005.14165*.

William Chan, Chitwan Saharia, Geoffrey Hinton, Mohammad Norouzi, and Navdeep Jaitly. 2020. Imputer: Sequence modelling via imputation and dynamic programming. In *International Conference on Machine Learning*, pages 1403–1413. PMLR.

Nanxin Chen, Shinji Watanabe, Jesús Villalba, and Najim Dehak. 2019. Listen and fill in the missing letters: Non-autoregressive transformer for speech recognition. *arXiv preprint arXiv:1911.04908*.

Yuntian Deng and Alexander Rush. 2020. Cascaded text generation with markov transformers. *Advances in Neural Information Processing Systems*, 33.

Liang Ding, Longyue Wang, Xuebo Liu, Derek F Wong, Dacheng Tao, and Zhaopeng Tu. 2020. Understanding and improving lexical choice in non-autoregressive translation. *arXiv preprint arXiv:2012.14583*.

Cunxiao Du, Zhaopeng Tu, and Jing Jiang. 2021. Order-agnostic cross entropy for non-autoregressive machine translation. *arXiv preprint arXiv:2106.05093*.

Marjan Ghazvininejad, Vladimir Karpukhin, Luke Zettlemoyer, and Omer Levy. 2020a. Aligned cross entropy for non-autoregressive machine translation. In *International Conference on Machine Learning*, pages 3515–3523. PMLR.

Marjan Ghazvininejad, Omer Levy, Yinhan Liu, and Luke Zettlemoyer. 2019. Mask-predict: Parallel decoding of conditional masked language models. In *Proceedings of the 2019 Conference on Empirical Methods in Natural Language Processing and the 9th International Joint Conference on Natural Language Processing (EMNLP-IJCNLP)*, pages 6114–6123.

Marjan Ghazvininejad, Omer Levy, and Luke Zettlemoyer. 2020b. Semi-autoregressive training improves mask-predict decoding. *arXiv preprint arXiv:2001.08785*.

Alex Graves, Santiago Fernández, Faustino Gomez, and Jürgen Schmidhuber. 2006. Connectionist temporal classification: Labelling unsegmented sequence data with recurrent neural networks. In *Proceedings of the 23rd International Conference on Machine Learning*, ICML '06, page 369–376, New York, NY, USA. Association for Computing Machinery.

Jiatao Gu, James Bradbury, Caiming Xiong, Victor OK Li, and Richard Socher. 2018. Non-autoregressive neural machine translation. In *International Conference on Learning Representations*.

Jiatao Gu and Xiang Kong. 2021. Fully non-autoregressive neural machine translation: Tricks of the trade. In *Findings of the Association for Computational Linguistics: ACL-IJCNLP 2021*, pages 120–133, Online. Association for Computational Linguistics.

Jiatao Gu, Changhan Wang, and Junbo Zhao. 2019. Levenshtein transformer. In *Advances in Neural Information Processing Systems*, volume 32, pages 11181–11191. Curran Associates, Inc.

Junliang Guo, Xu Tan, Di He, Tao Qin, Linli Xu, and Tie-Yan Liu. 2019. Non-autoregressive neural machine translation with enhanced decoder input. In *Proceedings of the AAAI Conference on Artificial Intelligence*, volume 33, pages 3723–3730.

Junliang Guo, Xu Tan, Linli Xu, Tao Qin, Enhong Chen, and Tie-Yan Liu. 2020a. Fine-tuning by curriculum learning for non-autoregressive neural machine translation. In *Proceedings of the AAAI Conference on Artificial Intelligence*, volume 34, pages 7839–7846.

Junliang Guo, Linli Xu, and Enhong Chen. 2020b. Jointly masked sequence-to-sequence model for non-autoregressive neural machine translation. In *Proceedings of the 58th Annual Meeting of the Association for Computational Linguistics*, pages 376–385.

Tomoki Hayashi, Wen-Chin Huang, Kazuhiro Kobayashi, and Tomoki Toda. 2021. Non-autoregressive sequence-to-sequence voice conversion. In *ICASSP 2021-2021 IEEE International Conference on Acoustics, Speech and Signal Processing (ICASSP)*, pages 7068–7072. IEEE.

Yosuke Higuchi, Shinji Watanabe, Nanxin Chen, Tetsuji Ogawa, and Tetsunori Kobayashi. 2020. Mask ctc: Non-autoregressive end-to-end asr with ctc and mask predict. *arXiv preprint arXiv:2005.08700*.

Po-Sen Huang, Chong Wang, Sitao Huang, Dengyong Zhou, and Li Deng. 2017. Towards neural phrase-based machine translation. *CoRR*, abs/1706.05565.

Ting Jiang, Shaohan Huang, Zihan Zhang, Deqing Wang, Fuzhen Zhuang, Furu Wei, Haizhen Huang, Liangjie Zhang, and Qi Zhang. 2021. Improving non-autoregressive generation with mixup training. *arXiv preprint arXiv:2110.11115*.

Kaggle. 2019. Deepfake detection challenge | kaggle. https://www.kaggle.com/c/deepfake-detection-challenge.

Lukasz Kaiser, Samy Bengio, Aurko Roy, Ashish Vaswani, Niki Parmar, Jakob Uszkoreit, and Noam Shazeer. 2018. Fast decoding in sequence models using discrete latent variables. In *International Conference on Machine Learning*, pages 2395–2404.

Hirokazu Kameoka, Kou Tanaka, and Takuhiro Kaneko. 2021. Fasts2s-vc: Streaming non-autoregressive sequence-to-sequence voice conversion. *arXiv preprint arXiv:2104.06900*.

Jungo Kasai, James Cross, Marjan Ghazvininejad, and Jiatao Gu. 2020. Non-autoregressive machine translation with disentangled context transformer. In *International Conference on Machine Learning*, pages 5144–5155. PMLR.

Jaehyeon Kim, Sungwon Kim, Jungil Kong, and Sungroh Yoon. 2020. Glow-tts: A generative flow for text-to-speech via monotonic alignment search. *Advances in Neural Information Processing Systems*, 33.

Jaehyeon Kim, Jungil Kong, and Juhee Son. 2021. Conditional variational autoencoder with adversarial learning for end-to-end text-to-speech. *arXiv preprint arXiv:2106.06103*.

Yoon Kim and Alexander M Rush. 2016. Sequence-level knowledge distillation. In *Proceedings of the 2016 Conference on Empirical Methods in Natural Language Processing*, pages 1317–1327.

Jungil Kong, Jaehyeon Kim, and Jaekyoung Bae. 2020a. Hifi-gan: Generative adversarial networks for efficient and high fidelity speech synthesis. *Advances in Neural Information Processing Systems*, 33.

Xiang Kong, Zhisong Zhang, and Eduard Hovy. 2020b. Incorporating a local translation mechanism into non-autoregressive translation. In *Proceedings of the 2020 Conference on Empirical Methods in Natural Language Processing (EMNLP)*, pages 1067–1073, Online. Association for Computational Linguistics.

John D. Lafferty, Andrew McCallum, and Fernando C. N. Pereira. 2001. Conditional random fields: Probabilistic models for segmenting and labeling sequence data. In *Proceedings of the Eighteenth International Conference on Machine Learning*, ICML '01, page 282–289, San Francisco, CA, USA. Morgan Kaufmann Publishers Inc.

Jason Lee, Elman Mansimov, and Kyunghyun Cho. 2018. Deterministic non-autoregressive neural sequence modeling by iterative refinement. In *Proceedings of the 2018 Conference on Empirical Methods in Natural Language Processing, Brussels, Belgium, October 31 - November 4, 2018*, pages 1173–1182.

Jason Lee, Raphael Shu, and Kyunghyun Cho. 2020. Iterative refinement in the continuous space for non-autoregressive neural machine translation. In *Proceedings of the 2020 Conference on Empirical Methods in Natural Language Processing (EMNLP)*, pages 1006–1015.

Yichong Leng, Xu Tan, Rui Wang, Linchen Zhu, Jin Xu, Linquan Liu, Tao Qin, Xiang-Yang Li, Edward Lin, and Tie-Yan Liu. 2021a. Fastcorrect 2: Fast error correction on multiple candidates for automatic speech recognition. *arXiv preprint arXiv:2109.14420*.

Yichong Leng, Xu Tan, Linchen Zhu, Jin Xu, Renqian Luo, Linquan Liu, Tao Qin, Xiang-Yang Li, Ed Lin, and Tie-Yan Liu. 2021b. Fastcorrect: Fast error correction with edit alignment for automatic speech recognition. In *NeurIPS*.

Jindřich Libovický and Jindřich Helcl. 2018. End-to-end non-autoregressive neural machine translation with connectionist temporal classification. In *Proceedings of the 2018 Conference on Empirical Methods in Natural Language Processing*, pages 3016–3021, Brussels, Belgium. Association for Computational Linguistics.

Guangyi Liu, Zichao Yang, Tianhua Tao, Xiaodan Liang, Zhen Li, Bowen Zhou, Shuguang Cui, and Zhiting Hu. 2021. Don't take it literally: An edit-invariant sequence loss for text generation. *arXiv preprint arXiv:2106.15078*.

Jinglin Liu, Yi Ren, Xu Tan, Chen Zhang, Tao Qin, Zhou Zhao, and Tie-Yan Liu. 2020. Task-level curriculum learning for non-autoregressive neural machine translation. *arXiv preprint arXiv:2007.08772*.

Mingbo Ma, Liang Huang, Hao Xiong, Renjie Zheng, Kaibo Liu, Baigong Zheng, Chuanqiang Zhang, Zhongjun He, Hairong Liu, Xing Li, et al. 2019a. Stacl: Simultaneous translation with implicit anticipation and controllable latency using prefix-to-prefix framework. In *Proceedings of the 57th Annual Meeting of the Association for Computational Linguistics*, pages 3025–3036.

Xuezhe Ma, Chunting Zhou, Xian Li, Graham Neubig, and Eduard Hovy. 2019b. Flowseq: Non-autoregressive conditional sequence generation with generative flow. *arXiv preprint arXiv:1909.02480*.

Jonathan Mallinson, Aliaksei Severyn, Eric Malmi, and Guillermo Garrido. 2020. Felix: Flexible text editing through tagging and insertion. In *Proceedings of the 2020 Conference on Empirical Methods in Natural Language Processing: Findings*, pages 1244–1255.

Aaron Oord, Yazhe Li, Igor Babuschkin, Karen Simonyan, Oriol Vinyals, Koray Kavukcuoglu, George Driessche, Edward Lockhart, Luis Cobo, Florian Stimberg, et al. 2018. Parallel wavenet: Fast high-fidelity speech synthesis. In *International conference on machine learning*, pages 3918–3926. PMLR.

Kainan Peng, Wei Ping, Zhao Song, and Kexin Zhao. 2020. Non-autoregressive neural text-to-speech. In *International conference on machine learning*, pages 7586–7598. PMLR.

Weizhen Qi, Yeyun Gong, Jian Jiao, Yu Yan, Weizhu Chen, Dayiheng Liu, Kewen Tang, Houqiang Li, Jiusheng Chen, Ruofei Zhang, et al. 2021. Bang: Bridging autoregressive and non-autoregressive generation with large scale pretraining. In *International Conference on Machine Learning*, pages 8630–8639. PMLR.

Lihua Qian, Hao Zhou, Yu Bao, Mingxuan Wang, Lin Qiu, Weinan Zhang, Yong Yu, and Lei Li. 2020. Glancing transformer for non-autoregressive neural machine translation. *arXiv preprint arXiv:2008.07905*.

Yi Ren, Jinglin Liu, Xu Tan, Zhou Zhao, Sheng Zhao, and Tie-Yan Liu. 2020. A study of non-autoregressive model for sequence generation. *arXiv preprint arXiv:2004.10454*.

Yi Ren, Yangjun Ruan, Xu Tan, Tao Qin, Sheng Zhao, Zhou Zhao, and Tie-Yan Liu. 2019. Fastspeech: fast, robust and controllable text to speech. In *Proceedings of the 33rd International Conference on Neural Information Processing Systems*, pages 3171–3180.

Aurko Roy, Ashish Vaswani, Arvind Neelakantan, and Niki Parmar. 2018. Theory and experiments on vector quantized autoencoders. *arXiv preprint arXiv:1805.11063*.

Chitwan Saharia, William Chan, Saurabh Saxena, and Mohammad Norouzi. 2020. Non-autoregressive machine translation with latent alignments. In *Proceedings of the 2020 Conference on Empirical Methods in Natural Language Processing (EMNLP)*, pages 1098–1108, Online. Association for Computational Linguistics.

Chenze Shao, Yang Feng, Jinchao Zhang, Fandong Meng, Xilin Chen, and Jie Zhou. 2019. Retrieving sequential information for non-autoregressive neural machine translation. In *Proceedings of the 57th Annual Meeting of the Association for Computational Linguistics*, pages 3013–3024.

Chenze Shao, Jinchao Zhang, Yang Feng, Fandong Meng, and Jie Zhou. 2020. Minimizing the bag-of-ngrams difference for non-autoregressive neural machine translation. In *Proceedings of the AAAI Conference on Artificial Intelligence*, volume 34, pages 198–205.

Raphael Shu, Jason Lee, Hideki Nakayama, and Kyunghyun Cho. 2020. Latent-variable non-autoregressive neural machine translation with deterministic inference using a delta posterior.

Mitchell Stern, William Chan, Jamie Kiros, and Jakob Uszkoreit. 2019. Insertion transformer: Flexible sequence generation via insertion operations. In *Proceedings of the 36th International Conference on Machine Learning*, volume 97 of *Proceedings of Machine Learning Research*, pages 5976–5985, Long Beach, California, USA. PMLR.

Mitchell Stern, Noam Shazeer, and Jakob Uszkoreit. 2018. Blockwise parallel decoding for deep autoregressive models. In *Advances in Neural Information Processing Systems*, pages 10107–10116.

Zhiqing Sun, Zhuohan Li, Haoqing Wang, Di He, Zi Lin, and Zhihong Deng. 2019. Fast structured decoding for sequence models. In *Advances in Neural Information Processing Systems*, pages 3016–3026.

Justus Thies, Michael Zollhofer, Marc Stamminger, Christian Theobalt, and Matthias Nießner. 2016. Face2face: Real-time face capture and reenactment of rgb videos. In *Proceedings of the IEEE conference on computer vision and pattern recognition*, pages 2387–2395.

Lifu Tu, Richard Yuanzhe Pang, Sam Wiseman, and Kevin Gimpel. 2020. ENGINE: Energy-based inference networks for non-autoregressive machine translation. In *Proceedings of the 58th Annual Meeting of the Association for Computational Linguistics*, pages 2819–2826, Online. Association for Computational Linguistics.

Ashish Vaswani, Noam Shazeer, Niki Parmar, Jakob Uszkoreit, Llion Jones, Aidan N. Gomez, Lukasz Kaiser, and Illia Polosukhin. 2017. Attention is all you need. In *Proceedings of the Annual Conference on Neural Information Processing Systems (NIPS)*.

Chunqi Wang, Ji Zhang, and Haiqing Chen. 2018. Semi-autoregressive neural machine translation. In *Proceedings of the 2018 Conference on Empirical Methods in Natural Language Processing*, pages 479–488.

Weijia Xu, Shuming Ma, Dongdong Zhang, and Marine Carpuat. 2021. How does distilled data complexity impact the quality and confidence of non-autoregressive machine translation? *arXiv preprint arXiv:2105.12900*.

Chunting Zhou, Jiatao Gu, and Graham Neubig. 2020. Understanding knowledge distillation in non-autoregressive machine translation. *8th International Conference on Learning Representations, ICLR 2020, Addis Ababa, Ethiopia, April 26-30, 2020, Conference Track Proceedings*.

Learning with Limited Text Data

Diyi Yang[*] **Ankur P. Parikh**[†] **Colin Raffel**[◇]
[*]Georgia Tech [†]Google Research [◇]University of North Carolina, Chapel Hill

1 Introduction

Natural Language Processing (NLP) has achieved great progress in the past decade on the basis of neural models, which often make use of large amounts of labeled data to achieve state-of-the-art performance. The dependence on labeled data prevents NLP models from being applied to low-resource settings and languages because of the time, money, and expertise that is often required to label massive amounts of textual data. Consequently, the ability to learn with limited labeled data is crucial for deploying neural systems to real-world NLP applications. Recently, numerous approaches have been explored to alleviate the need for labeled data in NLP such as data augmentation and semi-supervised learning.

This tutorial aims to provide a systematic and up-to-date overview of these methods in order to help researchers and practitioners understand the landscape of approaches and the challenges associated with learning from limited labeled data, an emerging topic in the computational linguistics community. We will consider applications to a wide variety of NLP tasks (including text classification, generation, and structured prediction) and will highlight current challenges and future directions.

2 Tutorial Outline

This will be a **three-hour** tutorial devoted to the **cutting-edge** topic of *Learning with Limited Text Data*, divided into three sessions. Each session will be 40 minutes, followed by 10 minutes for Q&A and 10 minutes for a break. Each part includes an overview of the corresponding topic and widely used methods and a deep dive into a set of representative NLP work.

2.1 Data Augmentation

Data augmentation is a common technique used to artificially increase both the size (i.e. the number of datapoints) and the diversity (i.e. the deviation from the true data distribution) of a given training dataset. Small labeled training datasets often lead to overfitting, and data augmentation can help alleviate this issue by creating augmented data automatically or manually. Such techniques have been widely explored in the computer vision (CV) field, with methods like geometric/color space transformations, mixup, and random erasing. Although it is relatively challenging to augment textual data because of its complex syntactic and semantic structures, there exists a wide range of methods designed to augment text data.

Representative data augmentation methods in NLP include: *token-level augmentation* such as randomly deleting or masking tokens (Bowman et al., 2015), replacing words with synonyms or related words (Zhang et al., 2015; Kobayashi, 2018), and inserting or replacing non-important tokens with random tokens (Xie et al., 2017, 2019); *sentence-level augmentation* by paraphrasing (Roy and Grangier, 2019; Edunov et al., 2018) based on back-translation that first translates sentences into certain intermediate languages and then translates them back to generate paraphrases as intermediate languages with different vocabulary and linguistic structures like POS, syntax could introduce certain variance, round-trip translation (Xie et al., 2019; Coulombe, 2018), or generating sentences conditioned on given label; *adversarial data augmentation* that uses perturbed data to dramatically influence the model's predictions and confidence without affecting human judgements (Morris et al., 2020), such as finding neighbors in a model's hidden representations using gradients (Cheng et al., 2019) or concatenating distracting but meaningless sentences as the end of paragraphs (Jia and Liang, 2017); and *hidden-space augmentation* that manipulates the hidden representations through perturbations like adding noise or performing interpolations with other data points (Chen et al., 2020a).

Proceedings of the 60th Annual Meeting of the Association for Computational Linguistics: Tutorial Abstracts, pages 28 - 31

We will walk audiences through the recent widely-used data augmentation methods and use example NLP applications such as back-translation for unsupervised translation to demonstrate how to utilize these representative data augmentation techniques in practice.

2.2 Semi-supervised Learning

While data augmentation can be applied in the supervised setting to produce better results when only a small labeled training dataset is available, data augmentation is also commonly used in semi-supervised learning. Semi-supervised learning provides a way to leverage unlabeled data when training a model, which can significantly improve the models when there is only limited labeled data available. This is particularly useful in the common setting where unlabeled data is cheaper and easier to obtain compared to labeled data.

In this tutorial, we will briefly discuss various semi-supervised techniques explored by recent research in NLP using example applications or tasks. We group existing semi-supervised learning methods into different categories based on how they utilize unlabeled data: *Self-training* leverages supervision that inherently exists or can be automatically generated from the dataset (McClosky et al., 2006); *multi-task training* leverages extra auxiliary tasks with labels to further utilize unlabeled data related to the task of interest; and *consistency regularization* trains a model to output the same prediction when the input is perturbed through data augmentation (Sachan et al., 2019; Xie et al., 2019; Chen et al., 2020a,b).

2.3 Limited Data Learning for Low Resourced Languages and Future Work

There are other orthogonal directions for tackling the problem of learning with limited data, such as other methods for semi-supervised learning such as self-training (He et al., 2020), generative models (Cheng et al., 2016), and co-training (Clark et al., 2018). We will briefly discuss these methods, and more specifically, we will walk through audiences on how the aforementioned techniques can be leveraged for improving performance on **low-resource languages** as a case study, including cross-lingual transfer learning which transfers models from resource-rich to resource-poor languages (Schuster et al., 2019), few/zero-shot learning (Pham et al., 2019; Abad et al., 2020) which uses only a few examples from the low-resource domain to adapt models trained in another domain.

Despite the success of learning with limited data in recent years, there are still certain challenges that need to be tackled for better learning. To this end, we will conclude our tutorial by highlighting some of these challenges, including but not limited to the data distribution shift, quantify the diversity and efficiency of augmentation, dealing with out-of-domain unlabeled data, learning data augmentation strategies that are specific to text, and discussing future directions that may help advance the field.

2.4 Breadth

While we will give pointers to dozens of relevant papers over the course of the tutorial, we plan to cover around 7-8 research papers in close detail. Only 1-2 of the "deep dive" papers will come from the presenter team.

3 Diversity Considerations

This tutorial will cover techniques and topics beyond English as an application domain. We will also cover content around how learning with limited text data can be applicable to low-resourced language, dialects, and other related tasks. Our presenter team has a diverse background from both academia (a junior female faculty from Georgia Institute of Technology, and an assistant professor from University of North Carolina, Chapel Hill) and industry (a research scientist from Google). Our presenter team will share our tutorial with a worldwide audience by promoting it on social media. We will work with ACL/NAACL D&I teams, and consult resources such as the BIG directory to diversify our audience participation. Furthermore, we will engage with NLP initiatives like Masakhane that our team has connections to.

4 Prerequisites

The prerequisite includes familiarity with basic machine learning and deep learning models, especially those typically used in modern NLP, including attention mechanisms (Bahdanau et al., 2014), the Transformer architecture (Vaswani et al., 2017), sequence-to-sequence learning (Sutskever et al., 2014), etc. Furthermore, this tutorial assumes background in basic probability, linear algebra, and calculus. We will also provide a more paced introduction to the material with additional readings.

4.1 Reading List

1. An Empirical Survey of Data Augmentation for Limited Data Learning in NLP (Chen et al., 2021)[1];

2. MixText: Linguistically-Informed Interpolation of Hidden Space for Semi-Supervised Text Classification (Chen et al., 2020a)[2];

3. Understanding Back-Translation at Scale (Edunov et al., 2018);

4. Cross-lingual Language Model Pretraining (Conneau and Lample, 2019);

5. Parsing with Multilingual BERT, a Small Corpus, and a Small Treebank (Chau et al., 2020);

6. TextAttack: A Framework for Adversarial Attacks, Data Augmentation, and Adversarial Training in NLP (Morris et al., 2020);

7. Self-training Improves Pre-training for Natural Language Understanding (Du et al.)

5 Tutorial Presenters

Diyi Yang is an assistant professor at the School of Interactive Computing, Georgia Tech. Her research focuses on learning with limited and noisy text data, user-centric language generation, and computational social science. Diyi has organized four workshops at NLP conferences: Widening NLP Workshops at NAACL 2018 and ACL 2019, Casual Inference workshop at EMNLP 2021, and NLG Evaluation workshop at EMNLP 2021. She also gave a tutorial at the 2020 Chinese CSCW Summer School. She has taught courses on natural language processing at Georgia Tech since 2019.

Ankur Parikh is a senior research scientist at Google NYC and adjunct assistant professor at NYU. His research interests are in natural language processing and machine learning with a recent focus on high precision text generation. Ankur received his PhD from Carnegie Mellon in 2015 and has received a best paper runner up award at EMNLP 2014 and a best paper in translational bioinformatics at ISMB 2011. He has taught natural language processing at NYU since 2017.

Colin Raffel is an assistant professor of Computer Science at the University of North Carolina, Chapel Hill. His research is focused on machine learning algorithms for learning from limited labeled data, including semi-supervised, unsupervised, and transfer learning methods. His best-known work on the topics related to this tutorial include the T5 model and the MixMatch/ReMixMatch/FixMatch series of semi-supervised learning algorithms. He gave a tutorial at the 2017 International Society for Music Information Retrieval Conference[3] and has taught machine learning courses at UNC, Columbia University, and Google's TechExchange program.

6 Ethics Statement

We do not anticipate any ethical issues related to the topics of the tutorial.

References

Alberto Abad, Peter Bell, Andrea Carmantini, and Steve Renais. 2020. Cross lingual transfer learning for zero-resource domain adaptation. *ICASSP 2020 - 2020 IEEE International Conference on Acoustics, Speech and Signal Processing (ICASSP).*

Dzmitry Bahdanau, Kyunghyun Cho, and Yoshua Bengio. 2014. Neural machine translation by jointly learning to align and translate. *arXiv preprint arXiv:1409.0473.*

Samuel R Bowman, Luke Vilnis, Oriol Vinyals, Andrew M Dai, Rafal Jozefowicz, and Samy Bengio. 2015. Generating sentences from a continuous space. *arXiv preprint arXiv:1511.06349.*

Ethan C Chau, Lucy H Lin, and Noah A Smith. 2020. Parsing with multilingual bert, a small corpus, and a small treebank. *arXiv preprint arXiv:2009.14124.*

Jiaao Chen, Derek Tam, Colin Raffel, Mohit Bansal, and Diyi Yang. 2021. An empirical survey of data augmentation for limited data learning in nlp. *arXiv preprint arXiv:2106.07499.*

Jiaao Chen, Zichao Yang, and Diyi Yang. 2020a. Mixtext: Linguistically-informed interpolation of hidden space for semi-supervised text classification. *ACL.*

Luoxin Chen, Weitong Ruan, Xinyue Liu, and Jianhua Lu. 2020b. SeqVAT: Virtual adversarial training for semi-supervised sequence labeling. In *Proceedings of the 58th Annual Meeting of the Association for Computational Linguistics*, pages 8801–8811, Online. Association for Computational Linguistics.

[1] Collaboration from two of our tutorial presenters.

[2] Work from one of our tutorial presenters.

[3] https://colinraffel.com/talks/ismir2017leveraging.pdf

Yong Cheng, Lu Jiang, and Wolfgang Macherey. 2019. Robust neural machine translation with doubly adversarial inputs. *Proceedings of the 57th Annual Meeting of the Association for Computational Linguistics*.

Yong Cheng, Wei Xu, Zhongjun He, Wei He, Hua Wu, Maosong Sun, and Yang Liu. 2016. Semi-supervised learning for neural machine translation. In *Proceedings of the 54th Annual Meeting of the Association for Computational Linguistics (Volume 1: Long Papers)*.

Kevin Clark, Minh-Thang Luong, Christopher D. Manning, and Quoc Le. 2018. Semi-supervised sequence modeling with cross-view training. In *Proceedings of the 2018 Conference on Empirical Methods in Natural Language Processing*, pages 1914–1925, Brussels, Belgium. Association for Computational Linguistics.

Alexis Conneau and Guillaume Lample. 2019. Cross-lingual language model pretraining. In *Advances in Neural Information Processing Systems*, pages 7059–7069.

Claude Coulombe. 2018. Text data augmentation made simple by leveraging nlp cloud apis. *arXiv preprint arXiv:1812.04718*.

Jingfei Du, Edouard Grave, Beliz Gunel, Vishrav Chaudhary, Onur Celebi, Michael Auli, Veselin Stoyanov, and Alexis Conneau. Self-training improves pre-training for natural language understanding.

Sergey Edunov, Myle Ott, Michael Auli, and David Grangier. 2018. Understanding back-translation at scale.

Junxian He, Jiatao Gu, Jiajun Shen, and Marc'Aurelio Ranzato. 2020. Revisiting self-training for neural sequence generation. In *International Conference on Learning Representations*.

Robin Jia and Percy Liang. 2017. Adversarial examples for evaluating reading comprehension systems.

Sosuke Kobayashi. 2018. Contextual augmentation: Data augmentation by words with paradigmatic relations. *arXiv preprint arXiv:1805.06201*.

David McClosky, Eugene Charniak, and Mark Johnson. 2006. Effective self-training for parsing. In *Proceedings of the Human Language Technology Conference of the NAACL, Main Conference*, pages 152–159.

John X Morris, Eli Lifland, Jin Yong Yoo, and Yanjun Qi. 2020. Textattack: A framework for adversarial attacks in natural language processing. *arXiv preprint arXiv:2005.05909*.

Ngoc-Quan Pham, Jan Niehues, Thanh-Le Ha, and Alexander Waibel. 2019. Improving zero-shot translation with language-independent constraints. In *Proceedings of the Fourth Conference on Machine Translation (Volume 1: Research Papers)*, pages 13–23, Florence, Italy. Association for Computational Linguistics.

Aurko Roy and David Grangier. 2019. Unsupervised paraphrasing without translation. *arXiv preprint arXiv:1905.12752*.

Devendra Singh Sachan, Manzil Zaheer, and Ruslan Salakhutdinov. 2019. Revisiting lstm networks for semi-supervised text classification via mixed objective function. In *AAAI*.

Sebastian Schuster, Sonal Gupta, Rushin Shah, and Mike Lewis. 2019. Cross-lingual transfer learning for multilingual task oriented dialog. In *Proceedings of the 2019 Conference of the North American Chapter of the Association for Computational Linguistics: Human Language Technologies, Volume 1 (Long and Short Papers)*, pages 3795–3805, Minneapolis, Minnesota. Association for Computational Linguistics.

Ilya Sutskever, Oriol Vinyals, and Quoc V Le. 2014. Sequence to sequence learning with neural networks. In *Advances in neural information processing systems*, pages 3104–3112.

Ashish Vaswani, Noam Shazeer, Niki Parmar, Jakob Uszkoreit, Llion Jones, Aidan N Gomez, Łukasz Kaiser, and Illia Polosukhin. 2017. Attention is all you need. In *Advances in neural information processing systems*, pages 5998–6008.

Qizhe Xie, Zihang Dai, Eduard Hovy, Minh-Thang Luong, and Quoc V Le. 2019. Unsupervised data augmentation for consistency training. *arXiv preprint arXiv:1904.12848*.

Ziang Xie, Sida I Wang, Jiwei Li, Daniel Lévy, Aiming Nie, Dan Jurafsky, and Andrew Y Ng. 2017. Data noising as smoothing in neural network language models. *arXiv preprint arXiv:1703.02573*.

Xiang Zhang, Junbo Zhao, and Yann LeCun. 2015. Character-level convolutional networks for text classification. In *Advances in neural information processing systems*, pages 649–657.

Zero- and Few-Shot NLP with Pretrained Language Models

Iz Beltagy[†] **Arman Cohan**[†*] **Robert L. Logan IV**[‡] **Sewon Min**[*] **Sameer Singh**[‡]
[†]Allen Institute for AI, Seattle, WA [‡]University of California, Irvine
[*]Paul G. Allen School, University of Washington, Seattle, WA
{beltagy, armanc} @allenai.org
{rlogan, sameer} @uci.edu
sewon@cs.washington.edu

1 Introduction

The ability to efficiently learn from little-to-no data is critical to applying NLP to tasks where data collection is costly or otherwise difficult. This is a challenging setting both academically and practically—particularly because training neutral models typically require large amount of labeled data. More recently, advances in pretraining on unlabelled data have brought up the potential of better zero-shot or few-shot learning (Devlin et al., 2019; Brown et al., 2020). In particular, over the past year, a great deal of research has been conducted to better learn from limited data using large-scale language models.

In this tutorial, we aim at bringing interested NLP researchers up to speed about the recent and ongoing techniques for zero- and few-shot learning with pretrained language models. Additionally, our goal is to reveal new research opportunities to the audience, which will hopefully bring us closer to address existing challenges in this domain.

The detailed content of the tutorial is described in Section 2. The tutorial will start by motivating the challenge of learning from limited data, and providing an overview of historical few-shot NLP techniques. The tutorial will then start mainly focusing on recent few-shot learning methods using language models. It will cover methods from manual engineering, better inference algorithms to better tuning methods. We will then discuss the impact of different pretraining objectives, and meta-training strategies. Lastly, we will survey the current landscape of evaluation benchmarks, and their limitations. We will conclude the tutorial by suggesting open questions, and providing coding examples and web-based demonstrations instructing attendees how to easily use these methods using public resources.

2 Tutorial Content and Outline

This tutorial covers methods for zero- and few-shot learning with pretrained language models (LMs). The tutorial will be 3 hours long. Tutorial materials will be made available at: `https://github.com/allenai/acl2022-zerofewshot-tutorial`.

Introduction - (10 minutes) We will start by motivating why zero- and few-shot learning are important. In many situations, labelled data may be costly or otherwise difficult to procure. Language model finetuning, the predominant training paradigm in use today, exhibits poor performance in low-data regimes (Dodge et al., 2020). Furthermore, as LMs continue to grow in size, so do the associated costs of training and storing separate weights for each downstream task. Recent work on zero- and few-shot learning with pretrained language models can provide a potential solution.

Earlier work - (15 minutes) In the second section, we will review well-established methods for zero- and few-shot learning that do not necessarily use LMs, including data augmentation, semi-supervised learning, consistency training and co-training (Miyato et al., 2017; Clark et al., 2018; Xie et al., 2020; Chen et al., 2020).

Language models as few-shot learners - (20 minutes) In the third section, we will focus on few-shot approaches using LMs without any tuning. The fundamental observation in this section is that, by reformulating tasks as complete-the-sentence problems and potentially including training examples in-context, large pretrained language models can be used to solve NLP tasks without having to resort to finetuning. We will survey a few key papers, notably GPT-3 (Brown et al., 2020), and follow up work demonstrating the limitations of in-context learning (Perez et al., 2021). We will also discuss alternative approaches for calibrating and

Proceedings of the 60th Annual Meeting of the Association for Computational Linguistics: Tutorial Abstracts, pages 32 - 37
May 22-27, 2022 ©2022 Association for Computational Linguistics

scoring LM outputs (Zhao et al., 2021; Holtzman et al., 2021; Min et al., 2021).

Prompt-based finetuning - (25 minutes) In the next section, we will discuss prompt-based finetuning, which relaxes the restriction that the LM weights cannot be updated. We will introduce the technique of pattern exploiting training (Schick and Schütze, 2021a,b; Le Scao and Rush, 2021, PET) which utilizes manually written cloze style prompts in conjunction with language model finetuning to attain higher accuracy and improved stability over the finetuning approach proposed by Devlin et al. (2019). We will then discuss a variety of related works that seek to streamline PET (Tam et al., 2021; Logan IV et al., 2021). In particular we will cover methods that try to automate the task of prompt-construction, either in the vocabulary space (Shin et al., 2020; Gao et al., 2021b), or the embedding space (Li and Liang, 2021; Lester et al., 2021; Zhong et al., 2021; Qin and Eisner, 2021). We will contrast these methods with non-tuning methods covered in the previous section, in terms of their performance, memory and computation requirement, amount of required engineering, and more.

Pretraining - (20 minutes) The following section will focus on the factor underlying the success of these methods—language model pretraining. First, we will provide a review of popular language model pretraining objectives and architectures. Topics will include: causal (Radford et al., 2019) vs. masked (Devlin et al., 2019) pretraining, encoder-only (Devlin et al., 2019; Liu et al., 2019) vs. decoder-only (Radford et al., 2019) vs. encoder-decoder architectures (Lewis et al., 2020; Raffel et al., 2020), and the impact of training data (Aghajanyan et al., 2021; Saxton et al., 2019; Gao et al., 2021a).

Meta-training - (25 minutes) Next we will discuss meta-training approaches that train the LM to adapt to zero- and few-shot use cases. A variety of work has demonstrated that transfer learning is extremely effective when trained on a diverse set of tasks and prompts (Wei et al., 2021; Sanh et al., 2021). Furthermore, recent papers propose to learn from *instructions* where the model is given instructions that humans would often read when performing a new task, e.g., in a crowdsourcing task (Efrat and Levy, 2020; Mishra et al., 2021).

Evaluation benchmarks - (25 minutes) We will then discuss few-shot evaluation benchmarks such as FLEX (Bragg et al., 2021), FewNLU (Zheng et al., 2021), The BIG-Bench (BIG-bench collaboration, 2021) and CrossFit (Ye et al., 2021). We will discuss the problems in existing evaluations and how new few-shot evaluation benchmarks were carefully designed to measure a variety of scopes in generalization. We will also cover benchmarks specifically for instruction learning (Efrat and Levy, 2020; Mishra et al., 2021).

Open questions and future work - (20 minutes) The future work section will discuss open questions and future research directions like the need for multilingual evaluation data, challenges in evaluation, reducing engineering efforts and variance and more.

Coding example - (20 minutes) Finally, we will demonstrate code examples for representative few-shot methods using the most widely-used libraries/APIs at the time of the event, such as the Transformers library. This will help audience to easily use publicly available resources for real-world few-shot applications.

3 Type of the Tutorial

This tutorial will cover **cutting-edge** research in zero- and few-shot learning with pretrained language models. This topic has not been previously covered in *CL tutorials.

4 Breadth

The tutorial covers a diverse set of topics related to zero- and few-shot learning including pretraining, prompting, finetuning, evaluation, open research questions, etc. The tutorial also briefly discusses pre-language models work but not in depth. Note that most of the work we will cover is not authored by the presenters.

5 Diversity Considerations

The methods and techniques we are going to present are language-agnostic and can be easily applied to non-English data and tasks. Zero- and few-shot learning can be relevant for low-resource languages and tasks (assuming there exist unlabeled resources to build a pretrained model). The tutorial covers work from diverse groups, both geographically (America, Europe, Asia) and gender.

For instructors, three are senior and two are junior NLP researchers, one is female, and they represent two universities and one industry research lab.

6 Prerequisites

We assume attendees are familiar with:

- Machine Learning: Basic knowledge of common recent neural network architectures, particularly Transformers.

- Computational linguistics: Familiarity with the concept of pretrained language models, as well as standard NLP tasks such as text classification, natural language generation, and question answering.

7 Reading List

Reading the following papers is nice to have but not required for attendance.

- Language Models are Few-Shot Learners (Brown et al., 2020)

- It's Not Just Size That Matters: Small Language Models Are Also Few-Shot Learners (Schick and Schütze, 2021b)

- Finetuned Language Models are Zero-Shot Learners (Wei et al., 2021)

- FLEX: Unifying Evaluation for Few-Shot NLP (Bragg et al., 2021)

8 Instructors

In alphabetical order,

Iz Beltagy Iz Beltagy is a Research Scientist at AI2 focusing on language modeling, transfer learning, summarization, explainability and efficiency. His research has been recognized with a best paper honorary mention at ACL 2020 and an outstanding paper award at AKBC 2021. He was a co-instructor of the tutorial on "Beyond Paragraphs: NLP for Long Sequences" (NAACL-HLT 2021). He worked as a Teaching Assistant at the University of Texas at Austin teaching computer science.
Email: `beltagy@allenai.org`
Homepage: `beltagy.net`

Arman Cohan Arman Cohan is a Research Scientist at AI2 and an Affiliate Assistant Professor at University of Washington, focusing on representation learning and transfer learning methods, as well as NLP applications in specialized domains and scientific text. His research has been recognized with a best paper award at EMNLP 2017, an honorable mention at COLING 2018, and Harold N. Glassman Distinguished Doctoral Dissertation award in 2019. He was a co-instructor of the tutorial on "Beyond Paragraphs: NLP for Long Sequences" (NAACL-HLT 2021).
Email: `armanc@allenai.org`
Homepage: `armancohan.com`

Robert L. Logan IV Robert L. Logan IV is a Ph.D. student at the University of California, Irvine, advised by Sameer Singh and Padhraic Smyth. His research focuses on problems at the intersection of information extraction and language modeling, and encompasses recently published work on language model prompting that is relevant to this proposal. He has presented invited talks at the SoCal NLP Symposium (2019), the CHASE-CI Workshop (2019), and the UCI Center for Machine Learning Seminar (2021).
Email: `rlogan@uci.edu`
Homepage: `rloganiv.github.io`

Sewon Min Sewon Min is a Ph.D. student in the Paul G. Allen School of Computer Science & Engineering at the University of Washington, advised by Hannaneh Hajishirzi and Luke Zettlemoyer. Her research focuses on natural language understanding, question answering, and knowledge representation. She was a co-instructor of the tutorial on "Beyond Paragraphs: NLP for Long Sequences" (NAACL-HLT 2021), and was a co-organizer of the 3rd Workshop on Machine Reading for Question Answering (EMNLP 2021), Competition on Efficient Open-domain Question Answering (NeurIPS 2020), and Workshop on Structured and Unstructured KBs (AKBC 2020, 2021).
Email: `sewon@cs.washington.edu`
Homepage: `shmsw25.github.io`

Sameer Singh Sameer Singh is an Associate Professor of Computer Science at the University of California, Irvine and an Allen AI Fellow at the Allen Institute for AI. He is working on large-scale and interpretable machine learning models for NLP. His work has received paper awards at ACL 2020, AKBC 2020, EMNLP 2019, ACL 2018, and KDD

2016. Sameer has presented a number of tutorials, many relevant to this proposal, such as Deep Adversarial Learning Tutorial at NAACL 2019, Mining Knowledge Graphs from Text Tutorial at WSDM 2018 and AAAI 2017, tutorial on Interpretability and Explanations in NeurIPS 2020 and EMNLP 2020, and tutorial on Robustness in NLP at EMNLP 2021. Sameer has also received teaching awards at UCI.
Email: `sameer@uci.edu`
Homepage: `http://sameersingh.org/`

9 Ethical Statement

This tutorial covers work that extensively uses large (up to hundreds of billions of parameters) language models, which are associated with substantial financial and environmental costs (Strubell et al., 2019), as well as other harms (Bender et al., 2021).

References

Armen Aghajanyan, Dmytro Okhonko, Mike Lewis, Mandar Joshi, Hu Xu, Gargi Ghosh, and Luke Zettlemoyer. 2021. HTLM: Hyper-Text Pre-Training and Prompting of Language Models. *ArXiv preprint*, abs/2107.06955.

Emily M. Bender, Timnit Gebru, Angelina McMillan-Major, and Shmargaret Shmitchell. 2021. On the dangers of stochastic parrots: Can language models be too big? In *Proceedings of the 2021 ACM Conference on Fairness, Accountability, and Transparency*, FAccT '21, page 610–623, New York, NY, USA. Association for Computing Machinery.

BIG-bench collaboration. 2021. Beyond the imitation game: Measuring and extrapolating the capabilities of language models. *In preparation*.

Jonathan Bragg, Arman Cohan, Kyle Lo, and Iz Beltagy. 2021. FLEX: Unifying Evaluation for Few-Shot NLP. *ArXiv preprint*, abs/2107.07170.

Tom B. Brown, Benjamin Mann, Nick Ryder, Melanie Subbiah, Jared Kaplan, Prafulla Dhariwal, Arvind Neelakantan, Pranav Shyam, Girish Sastry, Amanda Askell, Sandhini Agarwal, Ariel Herbert-Voss, Gretchen Krueger, Tom Henighan, Rewon Child, Aditya Ramesh, Daniel M. Ziegler, Jeffrey Wu, Clemens Winter, Christopher Hesse, Mark Chen, Eric Sigler, Mateusz Litwin, Scott Gray, Benjamin Chess, Jack Clark, Christopher Berner, Sam McCandlish, Alec Radford, Ilya Sutskever, and Dario Amodei. 2020. Language models are few-shot learners. In *Advances in Neural Information Processing Systems 33: Annual Conference on Neural Information Processing Systems 2020, NeurIPS 2020, December 6-12, 2020, virtual*.

Jiaao Chen, Zichao Yang, and Diyi Yang. 2020. Mix-Text: Linguistically-informed interpolation of hidden space for semi-supervised text classification. In *Proceedings of the 58th Annual Meeting of the Association for Computational Linguistics*, pages 2147–2157, Online. Association for Computational Linguistics.

Kevin Clark, Minh-Thang Luong, Christopher D. Manning, and Quoc Le. 2018. Semi-supervised sequence modeling with cross-view training. In *Proceedings of the 2018 Conference on Empirical Methods in Natural Language Processing*, pages 1914–1925, Brussels, Belgium. Association for Computational Linguistics.

Jacob Devlin, Ming-Wei Chang, Kenton Lee, and Kristina Toutanova. 2019. BERT: Pre-training of deep bidirectional transformers for language understanding. In *Proceedings of the 2019 Conference of the North American Chapter of the Association for Computational Linguistics: Human Language Technologies, Volume 1 (Long and Short Papers)*, pages 4171–4186, Minneapolis, Minnesota. Association for Computational Linguistics.

Jesse Dodge, Gabriel Ilharco, Roy Schwartz, Ali Farhadi, Hannaneh Hajishirzi, and Noah Smith. 2020. Fine-tuning pretrained language models: Weight initializations, data orders, and early stopping. *ArXiv preprint*, abs/2002.06305.

Avia Efrat and Omer Levy. 2020. The Turking Test: Can Language Models Understand Instructions? *ArXiv preprint*, abs/2010.11982.

Leo Gao, Stella Biderman, Sid Black, Laurence Golding, Travis Hoppe, Charles Foster, Jason Phang, Horace He, Anish Thite, Noa Nabeshima, et al. 2021a. The pile: An 800gb dataset of diverse text for language modeling. *ArXiv preprint*, abs/2101.00027.

Tianyu Gao, Adam Fisch, and Danqi Chen. 2021b. Making pre-trained language models better few-shot learners. In *Proceedings of the 59th Annual Meeting of the Association for Computational Linguistics and the 11th International Joint Conference on Natural Language Processing (Volume 1: Long Papers)*, pages 3816–3830, Online. Association for Computational Linguistics.

Ari Holtzman, Peter West, Vered Shwartz, Yejin Choi, and Luke Zettlemoyer. 2021. Surface form competition: Why the highest probability answer isn't always right. In *Proceedings of the 2021 Conference on Empirical Methods in Natural Language Processing*, pages 7038–7051, Online and Punta Cana, Dominican Republic. Association for Computational Linguistics.

Teven Le Scao and Alexander Rush. 2021. How many data points is a prompt worth? In *Proceedings of the 2021 Conference of the North American Chapter of the Association for Computational Linguistics: Human Language Technologies*, pages 2627–2636, Online. Association for Computational Linguistics.

Brian Lester, Rami Al-Rfou, and Noah Constant. 2021. The power of scale for parameter-efficient prompt tuning. In *Proceedings of the 2021 Conference on Empirical Methods in Natural Language Processing*, pages 3045–3059, Online and Punta Cana, Dominican Republic. Association for Computational Linguistics.

Mike Lewis, Yinhan Liu, Naman Goyal, Marjan Ghazvininejad, Abdelrahman Mohamed, Omer Levy, Veselin Stoyanov, and Luke Zettlemoyer. 2020. BART: Denoising sequence-to-sequence pre-training for natural language generation, translation, and comprehension. In *Proceedings of the 58th Annual Meeting of the Association for Computational Linguistics*, pages 7871–7880, Online. Association for Computational Linguistics.

Xiang Lisa Li and Percy Liang. 2021. Prefix-tuning: Optimizing continuous prompts for generation. In *Proceedings of the 59th Annual Meeting of the Association for Computational Linguistics and the 11th International Joint Conference on Natural Language Processing (Volume 1: Long Papers)*, pages 4582–4597, Online. Association for Computational Linguistics.

Yinhan Liu, Myle Ott, Naman Goyal, Jingfei Du, Mandar Joshi, Danqi Chen, Omer Levy, Mike Lewis, Luke Zettlemoyer, and Veselin Stoyanov. 2019. RoBERTa: A Robustly Optimized BERT Pretraining Approach. *ArXiv preprint*, abs/1907.11692.

Robert L. Logan IV, Ivana Balažević, Eric Wallace, Fabio Petroni, Sameer Singh, and Sebastian Riedel. 2021. Cutting Down on Prompts and Parameters: Simple Few-Shot Learning with Language Models. *ArXiv preprint*, abs/2106.13353.

Sewon Min, Mike Lewis, Hannaneh Hajishirzi, and Luke Zettlemoyer. 2021. Noisy Channel Language Model Prompting for Few-Shot Text Classification. *ArXiv preprint*, abs/2108.04106.

Swaroop Mishra, Daniel Khashabi, Chitta Baral, and Hannaneh Hajishirzi. 2021. Cross-Task Generalization via Natural Language Crowdsourcing Instructions. *ArXiv preprint*, abs/2104.08773.

Takeru Miyato, Andrew M. Dai, and Ian J. Goodfellow. 2017. Adversarial training methods for semi-supervised text classification. In *5th International Conference on Learning Representations, ICLR 2017, Toulon, France, April 24-26, 2017, Conference Track Proceedings*. OpenReview.net.

Ethan Perez, Douwe Kiela, and Kyunghyun Cho. 2021. True Few-Shot Learning with Language Models. *ArXiv preprint*, abs/2105.11447.

Guanghui Qin and Jason Eisner. 2021. Learning how to ask: Querying LMs with mixtures of soft prompts. In *Proceedings of the 2021 Conference of the North American Chapter of the Association for Computational Linguistics: Human Language Technologies*, pages 5203–5212, Online. Association for Computational Linguistics.

Alec Radford, Jeffrey Wu, Rewon Child, David Luan, Dario Amodei, Ilya Sutskever, et al. 2019. Language models are unsupervised multitask learners. *OpenAI blog*, 1(8):9.

Colin Raffel, Noam Shazeer, Adam Roberts, Katherine Lee, Sharan Narang, Michael Matena, Yanqi Zhou, Wei Li, and Peter J. Liu. 2020. Exploring the Limits of Transfer Learning with a Unified Text-to-Text Transformer. *Journal of Machine Learning Research*, 21(140):1–67.

Victor Sanh, Albert Webson, Colin Raffel, Stephen H Bach, Lintang Sutawika, Zaid Alyafeai, Antoine Chaffin, Arnaud Stiegler, Teven Le Scao, Arun Raja, et al. 2021. Multitask prompted training enables zero-shot task generalization. *ArXiv preprint*, abs/2110.08207.

David Saxton, Edward Grefenstette, Felix Hill, and Pushmeet Kohli. 2019. Analysing mathematical reasoning abilities of neural models. In *7th International Conference on Learning Representations, ICLR 2019, New Orleans, LA, USA, May 6-9, 2019*. OpenReview.net.

Timo Schick and Hinrich Schütze. 2021a. Exploiting cloze-questions for few-shot text classification and natural language inference. In *Proceedings of the 16th Conference of the European Chapter of the Association for Computational Linguistics: Main Volume*, pages 255–269, Online. Association for Computational Linguistics.

Timo Schick and Hinrich Schütze. 2021b. It's not just size that matters: Small language models are also few-shot learners. In *Proceedings of the 2021 Conference of the North American Chapter of the Association for Computational Linguistics: Human Language Technologies*, pages 2339–2352, Online. Association for Computational Linguistics.

Taylor Shin, Yasaman Razeghi, Robert L. Logan IV, Eric Wallace, and Sameer Singh. 2020. AutoPrompt: Eliciting Knowledge from Language Models with Automatically Generated Prompts. In *Proceedings of the 2020 Conference on Empirical Methods in Natural Language Processing (EMNLP)*, pages 4222–4235, Online. Association for Computational Linguistics.

Emma Strubell, Ananya Ganesh, and Andrew McCallum. 2019. Energy and policy considerations for deep learning in NLP. In *Proceedings of the 57th Annual Meeting of the Association for Computational Linguistics*, pages 3645–3650, Florence, Italy. Association for Computational Linguistics.

Derek Tam, Rakesh R. Menon, Mohit Bansal, Shashank Srivastava, and Colin Raffel. 2021. Improving and simplifying pattern exploiting training. In *Proceedings of the 2021 Conference on Empirical Methods in Natural Language Processing*, pages 4980–4991,

Online and Punta Cana, Dominican Republic. Association for Computational Linguistics.

Jason Wei, Maarten Bosma, Vincent Y. Zhao, Kelvin Guu, Adams Wei Yu, Brian Lester, Nan Du, Andrew M. Dai, and Quoc V. Le. 2021. Finetuned Language Models Are Zero-Shot Learners. *ArXiv preprint*, abs/2109.01652.

Qizhe Xie, Zihang Dai, Eduard H. Hovy, Thang Luong, and Quoc Le. 2020. Unsupervised data augmentation for consistency training. In *Advances in Neural Information Processing Systems 33: Annual Conference on Neural Information Processing Systems 2020, NeurIPS 2020, December 6-12, 2020, virtual.*

Qinyuan Ye, Bill Yuchen Lin, and Xiang Ren. 2021. CrossFit: A few-shot learning challenge for cross-task generalization in NLP. In *Proceedings of the 2021 Conference on Empirical Methods in Natural Language Processing*, pages 7163–7189, Online and Punta Cana, Dominican Republic. Association for Computational Linguistics.

Zihao Zhao, Eric Wallace, Shi Feng, Dan Klein, and Sameer Singh. 2021. Calibrate before use: Improving few-shot performance of language models. In *Proceedings of the 38th International Conference on Machine Learning, ICML 2021, 18-24 July 2021, Virtual Event*, volume 139 of *Proceedings of Machine Learning Research*, pages 12697–12706. PMLR.

Yanan Zheng, Jing Zhou, Yujie Qian, Ming Ding, Jian Li, Ruslan Salakhutdinov, Jie Tang, Sebastian Ruder, and Zhilin Yang. 2021. FewNLU: Benchmarking State-of-the-Art Methods for Few-Shot Natural Language Understanding. *ArXiv preprint*, abs/2109.12742.

Zexuan Zhong, Dan Friedman, and Danqi Chen. 2021. Factual probing is [MASK]: Learning vs. learning to recall. In *Proceedings of the 2021 Conference of the North American Chapter of the Association for Computational Linguistics: Human Language Technologies*, pages 5017–5033, Online. Association for Computational Linguistics.

Vision-Language Pretraining: Current Trends and the Future

https://vlp-tutorial-acl2022.github.io/

Aishwarya Agrawal
University of Montreal,
Mila, DeepMind
aishwarya.agrawal@mila.quebec

Damien Teney
Idiap Research Institute
contact@damienteney.info

Aida Nematzadeh
DeepMind
nematzadeh@deepmind.com

1 Description

In the last few years, there has been an increased interest in building multimodal (vision-language) models that are pretrained on larger but noisier datasets where the two modalities (*e.g.*, image and text) loosely correspond to each other (*e.g.*, Lu et al., 2019; Radford et al., 2021). Given a task (such as visual question answering), these models are then often fine-tuned on task-specific supervised datasets. (*e.g.*, Lu et al., 2019; Chen et al., 2020; Tan and Bansal, 2019; Li et al., 2020a,b). In addition to the larger pretraining datasets, the transformer architecture (Vaswani et al., 2017) and in particular self-attention applied to two modalities are responsible for the impressive performance of the recent pretrianed models on downstream tasks (Hendricks et al., 2021).

This approach is appealing for a few reasons: first, the pretraining datasets are often automatically curated from the Web, providing huge datasets with negligible collection costs. Second, we can train large models once, and reuse them for various tasks. Finally, these pretraining approach performs better or on par to previous task-specific models. An interesting question is whether these pretrained models – in addition to their good task performance – learn representations that are better at capturing the alignments between the two modalities.

In this tutorial, we focus on recent vision-language pretraining paradigms. Our goal is to first provide the background on image–language datasets, benchmarks, and modeling innovations before the multimodal pretraining area. Next we discuss the different family of models used for vision-language pretraining, highlighting their strengths and shortcomings. Finally, we discuss the limits of vision-language pretraining through statistical learning, and the need for alternative approaches such as causal modeling.

We believe that the computational linguistics (CL) community will benefit from this tutorial in multiple ways. Language grounding research often uses or evaluates the most successful vision-language approaches. Better understanding of the shortcomings and strengths of these approaches – which we hope our tutorial provides – will pave the way for building stronger language grounding agents. Moreover, vision-language pretraining has been inspired by its parallel in pretraining language models. As a result, the CL community has a special role in thinking about the future of vision-language approaches using lessons learned from language pretraining.

2 Type of the Tutorial

This is a cutting-edge tutorial focusing on discussing the new trends in vision-language pretraining: if recent models result in better representations and how they contribute to downstream tasks. We plan to mostly discuss recent papers from 2018 and after but will also include influential papers from before 2018 that have played a crucial role in the current vision-language paradigms.

3 Target Audience

We expect the target audience to be researchers interested in the intersection of vision and language, such as the language grounding or grounded communication researchers. This tutorial is also of interest for junior students who are starting their career. Familiarity with recent architectures such as transformers is a useful but not needed for attending the tutorial.

4 Outline of the Tutorial

- Introduction: the goal of the tutorial (5 minutes)
- Vision-language landscape before the pretraining era (55 minutes)

Proceedings of the 60th Annual Meeting of the Association for Computational Linguistics: Tutorial Abstracts, pages 38 - 43

- Motivation for vision-language research from both application and research point of views.
- Popular vision-language tasks, datasets and benchmarks (e.g., image-retrieval, referring expressions, image captioning, visual question answering).
- Task specific modelling approaches and fundamental innovations before the pretraining era (e.g., CNN + LSTM based approaches, language guided image attention, multimodal pooling, compositional networks).

• Vision-language pretraining (VLP) (60 minutes)
    - Inspiration from pretraining successes in NLP (transformers, BERT, GPT).
    - Different families of VLP models (all are transformer based models):
        * Models using task-specific heads for each downstream task (e.g., ViLBERT, LXMERT, UNITER, OSCAR, VinVL).
        * Models treating all downstream tasks as language generation tasks, i.e. no task-specific head (e.g., VL-T5, VL-BART, SimVLM).
        * Models using VLP data for improving performance on vision tasks (e.g., CLIP, ALIGN).
        * Models using VLP data for improving performance on language tasks, including multilingual data (e.g., Vokenization, M3P, VL-T5, SimVLM).
    - Different VLP datasets and how they affect the downstream task performance w.r.t their size, degree of noise, and similarity with downstream datasets.

• Beyond statistical learning in vision-language (55 minutes)
    - Challenges yet to be tackled in vision-language research that are inherent limitations of the mainstream machine learning approach. These challenges include shortcut learning, sensibility of distribution shifts, model biases, adversarial vulnerabilities, and generally poor out-of-distribution generalization. We will also briefly cover privacy and fairness concerns when collecting large scale datasets, and the problem of models amplifying biases.
    - Background on causal reasoning necessary to formalize these issues and introduce potential solutions.
    - Existing benchmarks and other possible evaluation procedures that go beyond the traditional i.i.d. setting and allow diagnosing these issues: contrast examples, pairs of counterfactual examples, out-of-distribution test sets, etc.
    - Methods for learning better models by exploiting expert knowledge / inductive biases (Cadène et al., 2019; Ramakrishnan et al., 2018) or by utilizing different training paradigms (e.g., across multiple environments (Arjovsky et al., 2019; Teney et al., 2020b) or from pairs of training examples (Gokhale et al., 2020; Teney et al., 2020a)).

• Conclusion: main takeaways and future research (5 minutes)

5 Breadth of the Tutorial

We will mainly cover other people's work (as outlined in §4 and §7). More specifically, we expect the tutorial to include less than 15% of instructors' work – speakers will spend at most 10 minutes presenting their prior work.

6 Diversity Considerations

We are planning to increase diversity in a few ways: First, the topic of the tutorial is multidisciplinary bringing together researchers from diverse backgrounds (such as language, vision, and representation learning). We also plan to discuss how vision-language pretraining can benefit multilingual applications through grounding multiple languages into vision. Second, the instructors are from diverse backgrounds including their career stage (mid-career / junior), geography, gender, as well as their institution (academia / industry). Third, we will share our reading list, slides, and the recording of the talk publicly for people who cannot attend the conference in person, and also as a resource for junior researchers who are starting their career.

7 Reading List

- Popular vision-language tasks, datasets and benchmarks (Plummer et al., 2015; Kazemzadeh et al., 2014; Mao et al., 2015; Chen et al., 2015; Antol et al., 2015; Krishna et al., 2016; Hudson and Manning, 2019).

- Task specific modelling approaches before the pretraining era (Antol et al., 2015; Yang et al., 2015; Lu et al., 2016; Anderson et al., 2017; Fukui et al., 2016; Andreas et al., 2015).

- *Pretraining models in NLP (Devlin et al., 2018; Brown et al., 2020).

- VLP models with task-specific heads (Lu et al., 2019; Tan and Bansal, 2019; Chen et al., 2020; Li et al., 2020b; Zhang et al., 2021).

- VLP models without task-specific heads (Cho et al., 2021; Wang et al., 2021).

- VLP models for improving performance on vision tasks (Radford et al., 2021; Jia et al., 2021).

- VLP models for improving performance on language tasks (Tan and Bansal, 2020; Huang et al., 2020; Cho et al., 2021; Wang et al., 2021).

- Analyzing VLP models (Hendricks et al., 2021; Frank et al., 2021; Hendricks and Nematzadeh, 2021; Bugliarello et al., 2020).

- Shortcomings of vision-language models (Agrawal et al., 2016; Rohrbach et al., 2018; Gan et al., 2020; Ross et al., 2020; van Miltenburg, 2016; Misra et al., 2015; Raji et al., 2020; Zhao et al., 2017a).

- Methods and evaluation benchmarks that go beyond the traditional i.i.d. setting (Agrawal et al., 2017; Cadène et al., 2019; Ramakrishnan et al., 2018; Teney et al., 2020c; Arjovsky et al., 2019; Teney et al., 2020b; Gokhale et al., 2020; Teney et al., 2020a; Ilse et al., 2020; Agarwal et al., 2019).

* It would be great if the audience could read these papers before the tutorial, but it is okay even if they do not get a chance, as we will briefly cover these topics in the tutorial.

8 Instructors

Aishwarya Agrawal [webpage: `https://www.iro.umontreal.ca/~agrawal`] is an Assistant Professor in the Department of Computer Science and Operations Research at the University of Montreal. She is also a Canada CIFAR AI Chair and a core academic member of Mila – Quebec AI Institute. She also spends one day a week at DeepMind as a Research Scientist. Aishwarya's research interests lie at the intersection of computer vision, deep learning and natural language processing. Aishwarya is one of the two lead authors on the VQA paper (Antol et al., 2015) that introduced the task and the VQA v1.0 dataset. She has played an active role in releasing the dataset to the public. She is, in particular, keen about building vision-language models that generalize to out-of-distribution datasets. She used to co-organize the annual VQA challenge and workshop, and has given numerous invited talks (see `https://www.iro.umontreal.ca/~agrawal/index.html#talks`).

Damien Teney [webpage: `https://www.damienteney.info`] is a research scientist heading the machine learning group at the Idiap Research Institute in Switzerland. He is known for his work at the intersection of computer vision, machine learning, and natural language processing. He was part of the team that won the Visual Question Answering Challenge at CVPR 2017, which introduced the bottom-up/top-down attention mechanisms that are now ubiquitous for vision and language. His current research focuses on out-of-distribution generalization and learning methods inspired by causal reasoning. He has given multiple introductory talks on these topics and is a regular invited speaker at workshops and seminars on vision and language (e.g., VQA workshop at CVPR 2021, Vision and Language workshop at ACCV 2018).

Aida Nematzadeh [webpage: `http://www.aidanematzadeh.me`] is a staff research scientist at DeepMind. Her research interests are in the intersection of computational linguistics, cognitive science, and machine learning. Her recent work has focused on multimodal learning and evaluation and analysis of neural representations. She co-instructed a tutorial on "Language Learning and Processing in People and Machines" at NAACL 2019, and has given numerous invited talks (see `http://aidanematzadeh.`

me/talks.html).

9 Ethics Statement

Vision-language systems have many potential applications beneficial for society:

- Aiding visually impaired users in understanding their surroundings (Human: `What is on the shelf above the microwave?` AI: `Canned containers.`),
- Teaching children through interactive demos (AI captioning a picture of Dall Sheep: `That is Dall Sheep. You can find those in Alaska.`),
- Aiding analysts in processing large quantities of visual surveillance data (Analyst: `What kind of car did the man in red shirt leave in?` AI: `Blue Toyota Prius.`),
- Interacting with in-home physical robots (Human: `Is my laptop in my bedroom upstairs?` AI: `Yes.` Human: `Is the charger plugged in?`),
- Making visual social media content more accessible (AI: `Your friend Bob just uploaded a picture from his Hawaii trip.` Human: `Great, is he at the beach?` AI: `No, on a mountain.`).

But like most other technology, such vision-language systems could also be used for potentially harmful applications such as:

- Invasion of individual's privacy by using vision-language systems to query streams of video data being recorded by CCTV cameras at public places.
- Visually impaired users often need assistance with parsing data containing personal information (Ahmed et al., 2015), such as credit cards, personal mails etc. Vision-language systems providing such assistance could be configured to leak / retain such personally identifiable information.

In addition to the above potentially harmful applications of vision-language systems, there exist ethical concerns around fairness and bias. The vision-language models, as other deep learning based models (Zhao et al., 2017b), could potentially amplify the biases present in the data they are trained on. Since the training data (images and language) captures stereotypical biases present in the society (e.g, the activity of cooking is more likely to be performed by a woman than a man), amplification of such stereotypes by vision-language systems is concerning as it has the potential to harm the users in the relevant groups (based on gender, race, religion etc.) by entrenching existing stereotypes and producing demeaning portrayals (Brown et al., 2020).

To raise awareness about such ethical concerns and to promote discussions among researchers, the last part of the tutorial ("Beyond statistical learning in vision-language") will focus on such shortcomings of existing models and we will discuss some methods that aim to tackle some of these challenges.

References

Vedika Agarwal, Rakshith Shetty, and Mario Fritz. 2019. Towards causal VQA: revealing and reducing spurious correlations by invariant and covariant semantic editing. *CoRR*, abs/1912.07538.

Aishwarya Agrawal, Dhruv Batra, and Devi Parikh. 2016. Analyzing the behavior of visual question answering models. *CoRR*, abs/1606.07356.

Aishwarya Agrawal, Dhruv Batra, Devi Parikh, and Aniruddha Kembhavi. 2017. Don't just assume; look and answer: Overcoming priors for visual question answering. *CoRR*, abs/1712.00377.

Tousif Ahmed, Roberto Hoyle, Kay Connelly, David Crandall, and Apu Kapadia. 2015. Privacy concerns and behaviors of people with visual impairments. In *Proceedings of the 33rd Annual ACM Conference on Human Factors in Computing Systems*, pages 3523–3532.

Peter Anderson, Xiaodong He, Chris Buehler, Damien Teney, Mark Johnson, Stephen Gould, and Lei Zhang. 2017. Bottom-up and top-down attention for image captioning and VQA. *CoRR*, abs/1707.07998.

Jacob Andreas, Marcus Rohrbach, Trevor Darrell, and Dan Klein. 2015. Deep compositional question answering with neural module networks. *CoRR*, abs/1511.02799.

Stanislaw Antol, Aishwarya Agrawal, Jiasen Lu, Margaret Mitchell, Dhruv Batra, C. Lawrence Zitnick, and Devi Parikh. 2015. VQA: Visual Question Answering.

Martin Arjovsky, Léon Bottou, Ishaan Gulrajani, and David Lopez-Paz. 2019. Invariant risk minimization. *arXiv preprint arXiv:1907.02893*.

Tom B Brown, Benjamin Mann, Nick Ryder, Melanie Subbiah, Jared Kaplan, Prafulla Dhariwal, Arvind Neelakantan, Pranav Shyam, Girish Sastry, Amanda Askell, et al. 2020. Language models are few-shot learners. *arXiv preprint arXiv:2005.14165*.

Emanuele Bugliarello, Ryan Cotterell, Naoaki Okazaki, and Desmond Elliott. 2020. Multimodal pretraining unmasked: Unifying the vision and language berts. *CoRR*, abs/2011.15124.

Rémi Cadène, Corentin Dancette, Hedi Ben-younes, Matthieu Cord, and Devi Parikh. 2019. Rubi: Reducing unimodal biases in visual question answering. *CoRR*, abs/1906.10169.

Xinlei Chen, Hao Fang, Tsung-Yi Lin, Ramakrishna Vedantam, Saurabh Gupta, Piotr Dollár, and C. Lawrence Zitnick. 2015. Microsoft COCO captions: Data collection and evaluation server. *CoRR*, abs/1504.00325.

Yen-Chun Chen, Linjie Li, Licheng Yu, Ahmed El Kholy, Faisal Ahmed, Zhe Gan, Yu Cheng, and Jingjing Liu. 2020. UNITER: Universal image-text representation learning. In *European Conference on Computer Vision (ECCV)*.

Jaemin Cho, Jie Lei, Hao Tan, and Mohit Bansal. 2021. Unifying vision-and-language tasks via text generation. *CoRR*, abs/2102.02779.

Jacob Devlin, Ming-Wei Chang, Kenton Lee, and Kristina Toutanova. 2018. BERT: pre-training of deep bidirectional transformers for language understanding. *CoRR*, abs/1810.04805.

Stella Frank, Emanuele Bugliarello, and Desmond Elliott. 2021. Vision-and-language or vision-for-language? on cross-modal influence in multimodal transformers.

Akira Fukui, Dong Huk Park, Daylen Yang, Anna Rohrbach, Trevor Darrell, and Marcus Rohrbach. 2016. Multimodal compact bilinear pooling for visual question answering and visual grounding. *CoRR*, abs/1606.01847.

Zhe Gan, Yen-Chun Chen, Linjie Li, Chen Zhu, Yu Cheng, and Jingjing Liu. 2020. Large-scale adversarial training for vision-and-language representation learning. *CoRR*, abs/2006.06195.

Tejas Gokhale, Pratyay Banerjee, Chitta Baral, and Yezhou Yang. 2020. Mutant: A training paradigm for out-of-distribution generalization in visual question answering. *arXiv preprint arXiv:2009.08566*.

Lisa Anne Hendricks, John Mellor, Rosalia Schneider, Jean-Baptiste Alayrac, and Aida Nematzadeh. 2021. Decoupling the role of data, attention, and losses in multimodal transformers. *arXiv preprint arXiv:2102.00529*.

Lisa Anne Hendricks and Aida Nematzadeh. 2021. Probing image-language transformers for verb understanding. *CoRR*, abs/2106.09141.

Haoyang Huang, Lin Su, Di Qi, Nan Duan, Edward Cui, Taroon Bharti, Lei Zhang, Lijuan Wang, Jianfeng Gao, Bei Liu, Jianlong Fu, Dongdong Zhang, Xin Liu, and Ming Zhou. 2020. M3P: learning universal representations via multitask multilingual multimodal pre-training. *CoRR*, abs/2006.02635.

Drew A. Hudson and Christopher D. Manning. 2019. GQA: a new dataset for compositional question answering over real-world images. *CoRR*, abs/1902.09506.

Maximilian Ilse, Jakub M. Tomczak, and Patrick Forré. 2020. Selecting data augmentation for simulating interventions.

Chao Jia, Yinfei Yang, Ye Xia, Yi-Ting Chen, Zarana Parekh, Hieu Pham, Quoc V. Le, Yun-Hsuan Sung, Zhen Li, and Tom Duerig. 2021. Scaling up visual and vision-language representation learning with noisy text supervision. *CoRR*, abs/2102.05918.

Sahar Kazemzadeh, Vicente Ordonez, Mark Matten, and Tamara Berg. 2014. ReferItGame: Referring to objects in photographs of natural scenes. In *Proceedings of the 2014 Conference on Empirical Methods in Natural Language Processing (EMNLP)*, pages 787–798, Doha, Qatar. Association for Computational Linguistics.

Ranjay Krishna, Yuke Zhu, Oliver Groth, Justin Johnson, Kenji Hata, Joshua Kravitz, Stephanie Chen, Yannis Kalantidis, Li-Jia Li, David A. Shamma, Michael S. Bernstein, and Li Fei-Fei. 2016. Visual genome: Connecting language and vision using crowdsourced dense image annotations. *CoRR*, abs/1602.07332.

Gen Li, Nan Duan, Yuejian Fang, Ming Gong, and Daxin Jiang. 2020a. Unicoder-vl: A universal encoder for vision and language by cross-modal pretraining. In *The Thirty-Fourth AAAI Conference on Artificial Intelligence, AAAI*.

Xiujun Li, Xi Yin, Chunyuan Li, Xiaowei Hu, Pengchuan Zhang, Lei Zhang, Lijuan Wang, Houdong Hu, Li Dong, Furu Wei, et al. 2020b. Oscar: Object-semantics aligned pre-training for vision-language tasks. In *European Conference on Computer Vision*.

Jiasen Lu, Dhruv Batra, Devi Parikh, and Stefan Lee. 2019. Vilbert: Pretraining task-agnostic visiolinguistic representations for vision-and-language tasks. In *Advances in Neural Information Processing Systems*, pages 13–23.

Jiasen Lu, Jianwei Yang, Dhruv Batra, and Devi Parikh. 2016. Hierarchical question-image co-attention for visual question answering. *CoRR*, abs/1606.00061.

Junhua Mao, Jonathan Huang, Alexander Toshev, Oana Camburu, Alan L. Yuille, and Kevin Murphy. 2015. Generation and comprehension of unambiguous object descriptions. *CoRR*, abs/1511.02283.

Ishan Misra, C. Lawrence Zitnick, Margaret Mitchell, and Ross B. Girshick. 2015. Learning visual classifiers using human-centric annotations. *CoRR*, abs/1512.06974.

Bryan A. Plummer, Liwei Wang, Chris M. Cervantes, Juan C. Caicedo, Julia Hockenmaier, and Svetlana Lazebnik. 2015. Flickr30k entities: Collecting region-to-phrase correspondences for richer image-to-sentence models. *CoRR*, abs/1505.04870.

Alec Radford, Jong Wook Kim, Chris Hallacy, Aditya Ramesh, Gabriel Goh, Sandhini Agarwal, Girish Sastry, Amanda Askell, Pamela Mishkin, Jack Clark, et al. 2021. Learning transferable visual models from natural language supervision. *arXiv preprint arXiv:2103.00020*.

Inioluwa Deborah Raji, Timnit Gebru, Margaret Mitchell, Joy Buolamwini, Joonseok Lee, and Emily Denton. 2020. Saving face: Investigating the ethical concerns of facial recognition auditing. *CoRR*, abs/2001.00964.

Sainandan Ramakrishnan, Aishwarya Agrawal, and Stefan Lee. 2018. Overcoming language priors in visual question answering with adversarial regularization. *CoRR*, abs/1810.03649.

Anna Rohrbach, Lisa Anne Hendricks, Kaylee Burns, Trevor Darrell, and Kate Saenko. 2018. Object hallucination in image captioning. *CoRR*, abs/1809.02156.

Candace Ross, Boris Katz, and Andrei Barbu. 2020. Measuring social biases in grounded vision and language embeddings. *CoRR*, abs/2002.08911.

Hao Tan and Mohit Bansal. 2019. Lxmert: Learning cross-modality encoder representations from transformers. In *Empirical Methods in Natural Language Processing*.

Hao Tan and Mohit Bansal. 2020. Vokenization: Improving language understanding with contextualized, visual-grounded supervision. *CoRR*, abs/2010.06775.

Damien Teney, Ehsan Abbasnedjad, and Anton van den Hengel. 2020a. Learning what makes a difference from counterfactual examples and gradient supervision. *arXiv preprint arXiv:2004.09034*.

Damien Teney, Ehsan Abbasnedjad, and Anton van den Hengel. 2020b. Unshuffling data for improved generalization. *arXiv preprint arXiv:2002.11894*.

Damien Teney, Kushal Kafle, Robik Shrestha, Ehsan Abbasnejad, Christopher Kanan, and Anton van den Hengel. 2020c. On the value of out-of-distribution testing: An example of goodhart's law. *CoRR*, abs/2005.09241.

Emiel van Miltenburg. 2016. Stereotyping and bias in the flickr30k dataset. *CoRR*, abs/1605.06083.

Ashish Vaswani, Noam Shazeer, Niki Parmar, Jakob Uszkoreit, Llion Jones, Aidan N Gomez, Łukasz Kaiser, and Illia Polosukhin. 2017. Attention is all you need. In *Advances in neural information processing systems*, pages 5998–6008.

Zirui Wang, Jiahui Yu, Adams Wei Yu, Zihang Dai, Yulia Tsvetkov, and Yuan Cao. 2021. Simvlm: Simple visual language model pretraining with weak supervision. *CoRR*, abs/2108.10904.

Zichao Yang, Xiaodong He, Jianfeng Gao, Li Deng, and Alexander J. Smola. 2015. Stacked attention networks for image question answering. *CoRR*, abs/1511.02274.

Pengchuan Zhang, Xiujun Li, Xiaowei Hu, Jianwei Yang, Lei Zhang, Lijuan Wang, Yejin Choi, and Jianfeng Gao. 2021. Vinvl: Making visual representations matter in vision-language models. *CoRR*, abs/2101.00529.

Jieyu Zhao, Tianlu Wang, Mark Yatskar, Vicente Ordonez, and Kai-Wei Chang. 2017a. Men also like shopping: Reducing gender bias amplification using corpus-level constraints. *CoRR*, abs/1707.09457.

Jieyu Zhao, Tianlu Wang, Mark Yatskar, Vicente Ordonez, and Kai-Wei Chang. 2017b. Men also like shopping: Reducing gender bias amplification using corpus-level constraints. *arXiv preprint arXiv:1707.09457*.

Natural Language Processing for Multilingual Task-Oriented Dialogue

Tutorial Abstract

Evgeniia Razumovskaia[1], **Goran Glavaš**[2], **Olga Majewska**[1]
Edoardo Maria Ponti[4,5], **Ivan Vulić**[1,6]
[1] Language Technology Lab, University of Cambridge
[2] Center for Artificial Intelligence and Data Science, University of Würzburg
[4]Mila – Quebec Artificial Intelligence Institute [5]McGill University [6]PolyAI Limited
{er563,om304,iv250}@cam.ac.uk goran@informatik.uni-mannheim.de
edoardo-maria.ponti@mila.quebec

1 Motivation and Objectives

Enabling machines to intelligently *converse* with humans in order to solve particular well-defined *tasks* is in the core focus of task-oriented dialogue (ToD) systems and their development (Kim and Banchs, 2014; Li et al., 2018; Henderson et al., 2019; Zang et al., 2020). Such systems have wide applications in a multitude of domains such as hospitality industry, travel, e-banking, healthcare, entertainment industry, industrial production and maintenance, etc. ToD-oriented research has been recently catalysed by the growing ability and viability of deep learning techniques such as large-scale pretraining of language models (Ren et al., 2018; Wen et al., 2019; Henderson et al., 2020; Wu et al., 2020; Lin et al., 2020, *inter alia*). The momentum of development in this research area has, however, mainly targeted a very small proportion of potential beneficiaries: most existing ToD systems are predominantly built for English and a few other, major languages only (e.g., Chinese) (Lin et al., 2021; Ding et al., 2021). This limits the use, global reach, and transformative potential of ToD systems. Consequently, this deepens the chasm between speakers of dominant versus under-represented low-resource languages in their access to state-of-the-art language technology (Joshi et al., 2020; Blasi et al., 2021) and contributes to the digital language divide and inequality of information.[1]

Extending the reach of ToD technology is crucial for the democratisation and wide adoption of human–machine communication, with an inclusive long-term goal of bringing it to virtually *all* citizens of the world. Building on top of our recent comprehensive survey on the topic of *multilingual* ToD (Razumovskaia et al., 2021), in this tutorial our aim is to systematise the current research on multilingual ToD, and offer a fresh perspective to other researchers and NLP practitioners on the importance and challenges of developing multilingual ToD systems.

The tutorial will offer a comprehensive overview of multilingual ToD research and know-hows focused on the following central questions:[2]

(Q1) Why are multilingual ToD systems so hard to build? What are the main **roadblocks** and how can we facilitate their development? What are the main **design paradigms** of multilingual ToD?

(Q2) Which ToD **datasets** are currently available in one or more languages other than English? What are their strengths and weaknesses? How can we improve the current data design and collection efforts and protocols?

(Q3) What are the best **methods** and practices to incorporate language-specific information and perform target language adaptation for multilingual and cross-lingual ToD?

(Q4) How can multilingual ToD take inspiration from other **related fields** of NLP research to better tackle low-resource scenarios (e.g., cross-lingual transfer, injection of external knowledge into parameters of neural models)?

(Q5) How good are current (multilingual) ToD systems? Do automatic **evaluation** measures correlate with user satisfaction? What implication does multilinguality have on ToD evaluation?

(Q6) What are the **future challenges** faced when developing ToD systems in several different languages, especially with respect to voice-based and human-centered ToD?

2 Tutorial Overview and Structure

Part I: Introduction, Motivation, and ToD Preliminaries *(25 minutes)*

[1]http://labs.theguardian.com/digital-language-divide/

[2]All tutorial materials will be available at https://tinyurl.com/multilingualtod

Proceedings of the 60th Annual Meeting of the Association for Computational Linguistics: Tutorial Abstracts, pages 44 - 50
May 22-27, 2022 ©2022 Association for Computational Linguistics

Part I will cover the basics of modular and end-to-end dialogue systems (Young, 2010; Chen et al., 2017a; Wen et al., 2017; Ham et al., 2020), offering a brief overview of the full ToD system structure, and critical modules such as Speech-to-text/ASR, natural language understanding (NLU) for dialogue, dialogue state tracking (DST), dialogue management (DM), natural language generation (NLG), and text-to-speech (TTS), along with their functionality. We will analyse which components require language-specific processing and adaptation, and which modules are generally language-invariant. We will then proceed to define the detailed scope and schedule of the tutorial. Concretely, we plan to list and discuss all the current problems and challenges related to multilingual ToD development, and how we will introduce them in the subsequent tutorial parts. Topics overview:

- Main modules of ToD systems;
- Modular versus end-to-end ToD;
- Text-based (vs. other) ToD modules;
- Language-invariant vs. language-specific ToD modules;
- Why is development of multilingual ToD systems so difficult?

Part II: Methods and Resources for Multilingual *NLU* in ToD *(50 minutes)*

Part II will cover to-date work in multilingual NLU in ToD, including standard approaches and recent trends. We will provide a comprehensive overview of methods for learning cross-lingual representation spaces in ToD (Liu et al., 2019; Siddhant et al., 2020; Liu et al., 2020; Moghe et al., 2021) and their applications in different setups (multilingual vs. cross-lingual, zero-shot vs. few-shot). Finally, we will list available resources: those created specifically for multilingual ToD NLU (Ding et al., 2021; Zuo et al., 2021; Hung et al., 2022, *inter alia*) as well as external resources useful for ToD NLU. Part II comprises the following topics:

- Joint versus separate training for NLU: intent detection, slot labeling, DST;
- Learning shared cross-lingual representation spaces; from cross-lingual word embeddings to multilingual text encoders – how to leverage them for NLU in ToD?
- Multilingual (pre)training versus cross-lingual transfer methods;
- Zero-shot and few-shot learning scenarios;
- Datasets and resources: (a) for in-task dialogue training and (b) external resources (e.g., parallel data, bilingual dictionaries, multilingual knowledge bases).

Part III: Methods and Resources for Multilingual *NLG* in ToD *(35 minutes)*

Part III will present the methods for multilingual natural language generation and their usage for cross-lingual transfer of ToD. First, we will discuss traditional, grammar-based methods for cross-lingual generation (Gatt and Krahmer, 2018; Vaudry and Lapalme, 2013) and their combination with statistical methods (García-Méndez et al., 2019) for more efficient learning. Secondly, we will discuss cross-lingual transfer of ToD using machine translation (MT) in two ways: a) translating the test data into English ('translate test', Wan et al., 2010); b) translating the training data into the target language ('translate train', Duan et al., 2019), and how improvements in MT and multilingual pretraining affect cross-lingual transfer of ToD. Next, we will analyse the choice between retrieval-based, generation-based and hybrid ToD systems through the prism of multilinguality. Finally, we will address the difficulties of corpora creation for multilingual ToD generation. Topics:

- Traditional NLG and its extension to multiple languages;
- Retrieval-based versus generation-based versus hybrid approaches: pros and cons in multilingual setups;
- Leveraging shared cross-lingual representation spaces for multilingual NLG; translation-based approaches;
- Zero-shot and few-shot learning scenarios and language-specific adaptations;
- Available resources and datasets for multilingual NLG (for ToD).

Part IV: Evaluation of Multilingual ToD Systems *(30 minutes)*

Part IV will focus on evaluation for (multilingual) ToD. We will cover both automatic metrics and human evaluation: automatic metrics allow for faster development cycles, but often do not correlate with user satisfaction with ToD systems (Liu et al., 2016; Novikova et al., 2017). We will discuss the shortcomings of automated ToD evaluation, but also the potential pitfalls of human evaluation (Clark et al., 2021). We will then analyse the difficulties that multilingual setups pose for both automatic metrics and human evaluation, including evaluation of generated responses in morphologically rich languages and difficulty of finding qualified evaluators for rare languages. Topics:

- Current evaluation protocols in ToD;
- Automatic vs. human-centered evaluation in multilingual setups: pros and cons;
- How to evaluate language-specific phenomena and fluency;
- Difficulties in evaluation and current gaps in evaluation resources.

Part V: Open Challenges and Research Directions in Multilingual ToD *(40 minutes)*
In the concluding Part V, we will discuss the main open challenges impeding the development of ToD systems and reflect on the promising avenues for further progress. First, we will advocate for linguistically motivated design of multilingual ToD datasets focusing on linguistic diversity and idiomacity. To fulfill their role as gauges of model performance across languages (Hu et al., 2020; Liang et al., 2020), multilingual datasets should (i) maximise diversity along the dimensions of language family, geographic area, and typological features (Ponti et al., 2020). as well as (ii) adequately represent the linguistic and extra-linguistic (e.g., world knowledge, cultural references) properties of selected languages (rather than replicating dialogue structures, topics, and entities from a resource-rich source language). We will discuss first attempts at cultural adaptation for dialogue (Majewska et al., 2022). Second, we will outline how existing strategies for dealing with data scarcity can be borrowed from other NLP tasks to benefit multilingual and cross-lingual ToD NLU (Ponti et al., 2019; Hedderich et al., 2021). Third, we will emphasise the importance of user-centered evaluation as a way of assessing the fluency of generated responses and guiding improvements in ToD systems across different languages. Finally, we will discuss the significance of developments in multilingual ASR and TTS as keys to the ultimate success of multilingual ToD on a wide scale, and the potential of integrating speech-based and text-based modules in future research. Topics:

- Recommendations for creation of future multilingual ToD datasets: linguistic diversity and idiomacity, low-resource languages, expansion to new domains;
- Coping with low-resource scenarios: methods and lessons learned from other NLP tasks and applications; source selection for multi-source transfer and multilingual training;
- Fluency of generation, code switching;
- From text-based to voice-based multilingual ToD: promises and challenges;
- An overview of other related research areas that can benefit multilingual ToD;
- Listing key challenges, a short panel discussion and a QA session.

3 Tutorial Breadth and Diversity

According to the representative set of papers listed in the selected bibliography as well as in our recent survey paper (Razumovskaia et al., 2021), we anticipate that a total of 20%-25% of the tutorial concerns work which involves at least one of the five presenters. The rest of the tutorial will focus on providing a detailed comprehensive overview of the main topic by covering all the relevant work from other researchers: see again the wide bibliography and coverage in the survey paper.

Diversity and Inclusion. We consider the following aspects. First, our tutorial proposal focuses on multilingual NLP and promotes the ultimate long-term goal of NLP research: bringing (human-centered) language technology to minor and under-resourced languages, and acting as a vehicle of mitigating the *digital language divide* (see the footnote 1). As such, it is highly relevant to both special themes of ACL 2022 and NAACL-HLT 2022. Our tutorial will also expose prominent issues and gaps related to (lack of) diversity and inclusivity of current multilingual ToD models and datasets, and we hope to inspire research groups currently working separately on (i) ToD and (ii) low-resource languages and low-resource NLP to consider joining forces and research expertise in the future.

Concerning tutorial organization, we hope that our tutorial will connect researchers from different cultural backgrounds and research fields. We also note that two out of five tutorial presenters are female, and the pool of presenters offers a mix of more junior and experienced presenters.

4 Presenters

Evgeniia Razumovskaia is a PhD student in the Language Technology Lab at the University of Cambridge. She works on dialogue systems, focusing on efficient few-shot methods for multilingual dialogue systems. Web: `evgeniiaraz.github.io`

Goran Glavaš is a Full Professor (Chair for Natural Language Processing) and member of the

Center for Artificial Intelligence and Data Science (CAIDAS) at the University of Würzburg. His research focuses on multilingual representation learning and cross-lingual transfer (primarily for low-resource languages), fair and sustainable NLP, and NLP applications for social sciences and humanities. He has given tutorials at ACL 2019 and EMNLP 2019, organized workshops TextGraphs and SustainNLP, and served as reviewer and (senior) area chair for a number of *ACL events. He currently serves as an Editor-in-Chief for the ACL Rolling Review. Web: `sites.google.com/view/goranglavas`

Olga Majewska works at Amazon Alexa in Cambridge, UK, and an affiliated researcher at the Language Technology Lab, University of Cambridge, where she earned her PhD in computational linguistics in 2021. Her interests lie, among others, in multilingual expansion of conversational AI and development of efficient protocols for generation of task-oriented dialogue evaluation data for under-resourced languages. Web: `om304.github.io`

Edoardo Maria Ponti is a Visiting Postdoctoral Scholar at the University of Stanford and a Postdoctoral Fellow at MILA Montreal. He works on sample efficiency and modularity in neural networks, with applications to multilingual NLP. In 2020, he obtained a PhD in computational linguistics from the University of Cambridge, St John's College. Previously, he interned as an AI/ML researcher at Apple in Cupertino. His research earned him a Google Research Faculty Award and an ERC Proof of Concept grant. He received 2 Best Paper Awards at EMNLP 2021 and RepL4NLP 2019. Web: `ducdauge.github.io`

Ivan Vulić is a Senior Research Associate in the Language Technology Lab at the University of Cambridge, and a Senior Scientist at PolyAI. His research interests are in multilingual and multimodal representation learning, and transfer learning for low-resource languages and applications such as task-oriented dialogue systems. He has extensive experience giving invited and keynote talks, and co-organising tutorials (e.g., EMNLP 2017, NAACL-HLT 2018, ESSLLI 2018, ACL 2019, EMNLP 2019, AILC Lectures 2021) and workshops in areas relevant to this proposal (e.g., SIGTYP, DeeLIO, RepL4NLP, PC of *SEM 2021). For his contributions to NLP and IR, he obtained the 2021 Karen Spärck Jones award. Web: `sites.google.com/site/ivanvulic`

5 Prerequisites and Reading List

Math: no special requirements; *Linguistics*: basic knowledge of language typology and of morphology (recommended); *Machine Learning*: good grasp of core (supervised) machine learning concepts and familiarity with self-supervised pretraining of language models (required). Pre-tutorial reading list (examples):

- Wen, T. H., Vandyke, D., Mrkšić, N., Gašić, M., Rojas-Barahona, L. M., Su, P. H., & Young, S. 2017. A Network-Based End-to-End Trainable Task-Oriented Dialogue System. EACL 2017 (pp. 438-449).
- Blasi, D., Anastasopoulos, A., & Neubig, G. (2021). Systematic Inequalities in Language Technology Performance across the World's Languages. arXiv preprint arXiv:2110.06733.
- Razumovskaia, E., Glavaš, G., Majewska, O., Korhonen, A., & Vulić, I. (2021). Crossing the Conversational Chasm: A Primer on Multilingual Task-Oriented Dialogue Systems. arXiv preprint arXiv:2104.08570.

6 Other Tutorial Information

Related Tutorials. Conversational AI and (components of) ToD systems have been taught in several tutorials in past years, where the focus has been put on diverse aspects such as: deep learning techniques for ToD (Chen et al., ACL 2017; Su et al., NAACL-HLT 2018; Gao et al., ACL 2018), data collection and end-to-end learning (Wen et al., EMNLP 2019), or NLG methods (Ji et al., EMNLP 2020) and their evaluation (Khapra and Sai, NAACL-HLT 2021). However, our tutorial is the first to focus on the crucial aspects of multilingualism and low-resource languages in relation to the design, development, evaluation, and application of (multilingual) ToD systems. Our tutorial offers a completely novel and unique perspective to ToD also through the optics of multilingual NLP.

Ethical Considerations. ToD systems can and should be used for greater good, but their use also comes with potential harmful implications. As part of the tutorial, we will therefore also point to guidelines and required ethical standards related to ToD-oriented data collection and (user-centered) evaluation, and also provide an overview of potential threats in current ToD-oriented models (e.g., gender, race or religion biases (Barikeri et al., 2021)). Furthermore, we will remind NLP researchers and practitioners to bear in mind potential data- and model-centered biases, and apply appropriate data filtering and debiasing techniques before deploying ToD systems in real-world settings.

References

Soumya Barikeri, Anne Lauscher, Ivan Vulić, and Goran Glavaš. 2021. RedditBias: A real-world resource for bias evaluation and debiasing of conversational language models. In *Proceedings of ACL 2021*, pages 1941–1955.

Damián Blasi, Antonios Anastasopoulos, and Graham Neubig. 2021. Systematic inequalities in language technology performance across the world's languages. *arXiv preprint arXiv:2110.06733*.

Hongshen Chen, Xiaorui Liu, Dawei Yin, and Jiliang Tang. 2017a. A survey on dialogue systems: Recent advances and new frontiers. *SIGKDD Explorations*, 19(2):25–35.

Yun-Nung Chen, Asli Celikyilmaz, and Dilek Hakkani-Tür. 2017b. Deep learning for dialogue systems. In *Proceedings of the 55th Annual Meeting of the Association for Computational Linguistics: Tutorial Abstracts*, pages 8–14.

Elizabeth Clark, Tal August, Sofia Serrano, Nikita Haduong, Suchin Gururangan, and Noah A Smith. 2021. All that's 'human'is not gold: Evaluating human evaluation of generated text. In *Proceedings of ACL-IJCNLP 2021*, pages 7282–7296.

Bosheng Ding, Junjie Hu, Lidong Bing, Sharifah Aljunied Mahani, Shafiq R. Joty, Luo Si, and Chunyan Miao. 2021. GlobalWoZ: Globalizing MultiWoZ to develop multilingual task-oriented dialogue systems. *CoRR*, abs/2110.07679.

Xiangyu Duan, Mingming Yin, Min Zhang, Boxing Chen, and Weihua Luo. 2019. Zero-shot cross-lingual abstractive sentence summarization through teaching generation and attention. In *Proceedings of ACL 2019*, pages 3162–3172.

Jianfeng Gao, Michel Galley, and Lihong Li. 2018. Neural approaches to conversational AI. In *Proceedings of the 56th Annual Meeting of the Association for Computational Linguistics: Tutorial Abstracts*, pages 2–7.

Silvia García-Méndez, Milagros Fernández-Gavilanes, Enrique Costa-Montenegro, Jonathan Juncal-Martínez, and F. Javier González-Castaño. 2019. A library for automatic natural language generation of Spanish texts. *Expert Systems with Applications*, 120:372–386.

Albert Gatt and Emiel Krahmer. 2018. Survey of the state of the art in natural language generation: Core tasks, applications and evaluation. *Journal of Artificial Intelligence Research*, 61:65–170.

Donghoon Ham, Jeong-Gwan Lee, Youngsoo Jang, and Kee-Eung Kim. 2020. End-to-end neural pipeline for goal-oriented dialogue systems using GPT-2. In *Proceedings of ACL 2020*, pages 583–592.

Michael A. Hedderich, Lukas Lange, Heike Adel, Jannik Strötgen, and Dietrich Klakow. 2021. A survey on recent approaches for Natural Language Processing in low-resource scenarios. In *Proceedings of NAACL-HLT 2021*.

Matthew Henderson, Iñigo Casanueva, Nikola Mrkšić, Pei-Hao Su, Tsung-Hsien Wen, and Ivan Vulić. 2020. ConveRT: Efficient and accurate conversational representations from transformers. In *Proceedings of EMNLP 2020*, pages 2161–2174.

Matthew Henderson, Ivan Vulić, Inigo Casanueva, Paweł Budzianowski, Daniela Gerz, Sam Coope, Georgios Spithourakis, Tsung-Hsien Wen, Nikola Mrkšić, and Pei-Hao Su. 2019. Polyresponse: A rank-based approach to task-oriented dialogue with application in restaurant search and booking. In *Proceedings of EMNLP 2019*, pages 181–186.

Junjie Hu, Sebastian Ruder, Aditya Siddhant, Graham Neubig, Orhan Firat, and Melvin Johnson. 2020. XTREME: A massively multilingual multi-task benchmark for evaluating cross-lingual generalisation. In *Proceedings of ICML 2020*, pages 4411–4421.

Chia-Chien Hung, Anne Lauscher, Ivan Vulić, Simone Paolo Ponzetto, and Goran Glavaš. 2022. Multi^{2}WOZ: A robust multilingual dataset and conversational pretraining for task-oriented dialog. In *Proceedings of the 2022 Annual Conference of the North American Chapter of the Association for Computational Linguistics*, page *to appear*.

Yangfeng Ji, Antoine Bosselut, Thomas Wolf, and Asli Celikyilmaz. 2020. The amazing world of neural language generation. In *Proceedings of the 2020 Conference on Empirical Methods in Natural Language Processing: Tutorial Abstracts*, pages 37–42.

Pratik Joshi, Sebastin Santy, Amar Budhiraja, Kalika Bali, and Monojit Choudhury. 2020. The state and fate of linguistic diversity and inclusion in the NLP world. In *Proceedings of ACL 2020*, pages 6282–6293.

Mitesh M. Khapra and Ananya B. Sai. 2021. A tutorial on evaluation metrics used in natural language generation. In *Proceedings of the 2021 Conference of the North American Chapter of the Association for Computational Linguistics: Human Language Technologies: Tutorials*, pages 15–19.

S. Kim and R. E. Banchs. 2014. R-cube: A dialogue agent for restaurant recommendation and reservation. In *Signal and Information Processing Association Annual Summit and Conference (APSIPA), 2014 Asia-Pacific*, pages 1–6.

Anne Lauscher, Vinit Ravishankar, Ivan Vulić, and Goran Glavaš. 2020. From zero to hero: On the limitations of zero-shot language transfer with multilingual transformers. In *Proceedings of EMNLP 2020*, pages 4483–4499.

Xiujun Li, Yu Wang, Siqi Sun, Sarah Panda, Jingjing Liu, and Jianfeng Gao. 2018. Microsoft dialogue challenge: Building end-to-end task-completion dialogue systems. arXiv preprint arXiv:1807.11125.

Yaobo Liang, Nan Duan, Yeyun Gong, Ning Wu, Fenfei Guo, Weizhen Qi, Ming Gong, Linjun Shou, Daxin Jiang, Guihong Cao, Xiaodong Fan, Ruofei Zhang, Rahul Agrawal, Edward Cui, Sining Wei, Taroon Bharti, Ying Qiao, Jiun-Hung Chen, Winnie Wu, Shuguang Liu, Fan Yang, Daniel Campos, Rangan Majumder, and Ming Zhou. 2020. XGLUE: A new benchmark datasetfor cross-lingual pre-training, understanding and generation. In *Proceedings of EMNLP 2020*, pages 6008–6018.

Zhaojiang Lin, Andrea Madotto, Genta Indra Winata, and Pascale Fung. 2020. MinTL: minimalist transfer learning for task-oriented dialogue systems. In *Proceedings of EMNLP 2020*, pages 3391–3405.

Zhaojiang Lin, Andrea Madotto, Genta Indra Winata, Peng Xu, Feijun Jiang, Yuxiang Hu, Chen Shi, and Pascale Fung. 2021. BiToD: A bilingual multi-domain dataset for task-oriented dialogue modeling. *CoRR*, abs/2106.02787.

Chia-Wei Liu, Ryan Lowe, Iulian Vlad Serban, Mike Noseworthy, Laurent Charlin, and Joelle Pineau. 2016. How not to evaluate your dialogue system: An empirical study of unsupervised evaluation metrics for dialogue response generation. In *Proceedings of EMNLP 2016*, pages 2122–2132.

Zihan Liu, Jamin Shin, Yan Xu, Genta Indra Winata, Peng Xu, Andrea Madotto, and Pascale Fung. 2019. Zero-shot cross-lingual dialogue systems with transferable latent variables. In *Proceedings of EMNLP-IJCNLP 2019*, pages 1297–1303.

Zihan Liu, Genta Indra Winata, Zhaojiang Lin, Peng Xu, and Pascale Fung. 2020. Attention-informed mixed-language training for zero-shot cross-lingual task-oriented dialogue systems. In *Proceedings of AAAI 2020*, pages 8433–8440.

Olga Majewska, Evgeniia Razumovskaia, Edoardo Maria Ponti, Ivan Vulić, and Anna Korhonen. 2022. Cross-lingual dialogue dataset creation via outline-based generation. *arXiv preprint arXiv:2201.13405*.

Shikib Mehri, Mihail Eric, and Dilek Hakkani-Tur. 2020. DialoGLUE: A natural language understanding benchmark for task-oriented dialogue. arXiv preprint arXiv:2009.13570.

Nikita Moghe, Mark Steedman, and Alexandra Birch. 2021. Cross-lingual intermediate fine-tuning improves dialogue state tracking. In *Proceedings of EMNLP 2021*.

Jekaterina Novikova, Ondřej Dušek, Amanda Cercas Curry, and Verena Rieser. 2017. Why we need new evaluation metrics for NLG. In *Proceedings of EMNLP 2021*, pages 2241–2252.

Edoardo Maria Ponti, Goran Glavaš, Olga Majewska, Qianchu Liu, Ivan Vulić, and Anna Korhonen. 2020. XCOPA: A multilingual dataset for causal commonsense reasoning. In *Proceedings of EMNLP 2020*, pages 2362–2376.

Edoardo Maria Ponti, Ivan Vulić, Goran Glavaš, Roi Reichart, and Anna Korhonen. 2019. Cross-lingual semantic specialization via lexical relation induction. In *Proceedings of EMNLP-IJCNLP 2019*, pages 2206–2217.

Evgeniia Razumovskaia, Goran Glavas, Olga Majewska, Edoardo Maria Ponti, Anna Korhonen, and Ivan Vulić. 2021. Crossing the conversational chasm: A primer on multilingual task-oriented dialogue systems. *CoRR*, abs/2104.08570.

Liliang Ren, Kaige Xie, Lu Chen, and Kai Yu. 2018. Towards universal dialogue state tracking. In *Proceedings of EMNLP 2018*, pages 2780–2786.

Aditya Siddhant, Melvin Johnson, Henry Tsai, Naveen Ari, Jason Riesa, Ankur Bapna, Orhan Firat, and Karthik Raman. 2020. Evaluating the cross-lingual effectiveness of massively multilingual neural machine translation. In *Proceedings of AAAI 2020*, pages 8854–8861.

Pei-Hao Su, Nikola Mrkšić, Iñigo Casanueva, and Ivan Vulić. 2018. Deep learning for conversational AI. In *Proceedings of NAACL-HLT 2018: Tutorial Abstracts*, pages 27–32.

Pierre-Luc Vaudry and Guy Lapalme. 2013. Adapting simplenlg for bilingual english-french realisation. In *Proceedings of the 14th European Workshop on Natural Language Generation*, pages 183–187.

Xiaojun Wan, Huiying Li, and Jianguo Xiao. 2010. Cross-language document summarization based on machine translation quality prediction. In *Proceedings of ACL 2010*, pages 917–926.

Tsung-Hsien Wen, Pei-Hao Su, Paweł Budzianowski, Iñigo Casanueva, and Ivan Vulić. 2019. Data collection and end-to-end learning for conversational AI. In *Proceedings of the 2019 Conference on Empirical Methods in Natural Language Processing and the 9th International Joint Conference on Natural Language Processing (EMNLP-IJCNLP): Tutorial Abstracts*.

Tsung-Hsien Wen, David Vandyke, Nikola Mrkšić, Milica Gasic, Lina M Rojas Barahona, Pei-Hao Su, Stefan Ultes, and Steve Young. 2017. A network-based end-to-end trainable task-oriented dialogue system. In *Proceedings of EACL 2017*, pages 438–449.

Chien-Sheng Wu, Steven C.H. Hoi, Richard Socher, and Caiming Xiong. 2020. TOD-BERT: Pre-trained natural language understanding for task-oriented dialogue. In *Proceedings of EMNLP 2020*, pages 917–929.

Weijia Xu, Batool Haider, and Saab Mansour. 2020. End-to-end slot alignment and recognition for cross-lingual nlu. In *Proceedings of EMNLP 2020*, pages 5052–5063.

Steve Young. 2010. Still talking to machines (cognitively speaking). In *Proceedings of INTERSPEECH*, pages 1–10.

Xiaoxue Zang, Abhinav Rastogi, Srinivas Sunkara, Raghav Gupta, Jianguo Zhang, and Jindong Chen. 2020. MultiWOZ 2.2 : A dialogue dataset with additional annotation corrections and state tracking baselines. In *Proceedings of the 2nd Workshop on Natural Language Processing for Conversational AI*, pages 109–117.

Lei Zuo, Kun Qian, Bowen Yang, and Zhou Yu. 2021. Allwoz: Towards multilingual task-oriented dialog systems for all. *CoRR*, abs/2112.08333.

Author Index

Agrawal, Aishwarya, 38

Beltagy, Iz, 32
Bhargav, Samarth, 7
Bleeker, Maurits, 7

Chen, Zeyu, 1
Church, Kenneth, 1
Cohan, Arman, 32

Davis, Ernest, 1
Dodge, Jesse, 7

Forde, Jessica Zosa, 7

Glavaš, Goran, 44
Gu, Jiatao, 21

Jiang, Meng, 12

Kordoni, Valia, 1

Lin, Bill Yuchen, 12
Logan IV, Robert L., 32
Luccioni, Sasha, 7
Lucic, Ana, 7

Ma, Yanjun, 1
Majewska, Olga, 44
Marcus, Gary, 1
Min, Sewon, 32

Nematzadeh, Aida, 38

Parikh, Ankur P, 28
Ponti, Edoardo, 44

Raffel, Colin, 28
Razumovskaia, Evgeniia, 44
Ren, Xiang, 12

Singh, Sameer, 32
Sinha, Koustuv, 7
Stojnic, Robert, 7

Tan, Xu, 21
Teney, Damien, 38

Vulić, Ivan, 44

Xu, Yichong, 12

Yang, Diyi, 28
Yu, Wenhao, 12

Zhu, Chenguang, 12

Association for Computational Linguistics
209 N. Eighth Street
Stroudsburg, Pennsylvania 18360

ISBN 978-1-7138-6725-8

CURRAN ASSOCIATES INC.
proceedings.com

1st Workshop on Multilingual Multimodal Learning (MML 2022)

Dublin, Ireland
27 May 2022